THE UNIVERSITY C
WINCHESTF

# STATE LIABILITY

# STATE LIABILITY
## Tort Law and Beyond

CAROL HARLOW

**OXFORD**
UNIVERSITY PRESS

*in order to ensure its continuing availability*

# OXFORD
UNIVERSITY PRESS

Great Clarendon Street, Oxford OX2 6DP

Oxford University Press is a department of the University of Oxford.
It furthers the University's objective of excellence in research, scholarship,
and education by publishing worldwide in

Oxford  New York

Auckland   Cape Town  Dar es Salaam  Hong Kong   Karachi
Kuala Lumpur  Madrid  Melbourne  Mexico City   Nairobi
New Delhi  Shanghai  Taipei  Toronto
With offices in
Argentina  Austria  Brazil  Chile  Czech Republic  France Greece
Guatemala  Hungary  Italy  Japan  South Korea  Poland  Portugal
Singapore  Switzerland  Thailand  Turkey  Ukraine  Vietnam

ISBN 0-19-927264-6

# Acknowledgements

In writing this course of lectures, a version of which was given as the Clarendon Lectures in Oxford, in October 2003, I have received a great deal of help and encouragement. My thanks go first to the trustees of the Clarendon Lectures for their kind invitation, to the organizers, and especially Professor Peter Birks for his generous hospitality and that of All Souls. I am grateful too for the sponsorship of the Oxford University Press and to John Louth, their Academic Editor, responsible for the organization and subsequent publication of this volume.

The Lectures gave me the opportunity to return to the subject of government liability in tort, the subject of my PhD thesis, defended in 1980. Since those days, much has changed. I had kept up my interest in the subject and indeed I returned to it from time to time in books and articles, but no opportunity occurred for a sustained exploration of the changing landscape. That sustained work was on this occasion possible is due to the generosity of the Leverhulme Foundation and Mrs Jean Cater, who respectively awarded and administered a travelling Fellowship. This took me to Australia, where I am grateful for the hospitality of the Australian National University and its Research School of Social Sciences, which funded an extra month in Canberra. Particular thanks go to Peter Cane. The ANU Law School and Griffith University hosted seminars at which 'try out' papers were presented. Work on the European sections was conducted mainly at the European University Institute at Florence, where my thanks go in particular to head of department Jacques Ziller, but also in Paris at Sciences-Po, where Renaud Dehousse made the arrangements and entertained me. Keith Vincent, Kate Prichard, Shelley Brownlee, and, in New Zealand, David Dobbie competently did the research. Finally, thanks to the many colleagues who have discussed, read, listened, suggested, and provided information. My heaviest debts are to Mark Aronson, Peter Cane, and Jane Stapleton for general help, support, and advice. Peter kindly read the final text. Colin Scott and John Braithwaite advised on regulation and restorative justice, Takis Tridimas on EC law, and Duncan Fairgrieve on French law. With Leslie Zimans I endlessly debated the maverick case of *Stovin v Wise*. Lecture 2 is the product of endless and unresolved debate with Pavlos Eleftheriadis, James Penner, and Elspeth Guild.

My thanks to Richard Rawlings are of another order. In friendship and recognition of a long and profitable collaboration, these lectures are dedicated with great affection to Rick.

# Contents

Table of cases                                                    ix

**Introduction: Problem without Solution?**                       **1**

**1. Corrective Justice in the Frame**                            **10**
    Corrective Justice                        10
    Compensation: Towards a Tort Tax?         14
    Culpability and Deterrence                22
    Taking Dicey Seriously                    30
    Conclusion                                41

**2. Tort Law Abounding**                                         **42**
    The Cascade Effect of Globalization       42
    Accountability through Liability          49
    Responsibility and Liability              53
    Liability, Sanction, and the ECJ          56
    The Strasbourg Court and Satisfaction:
        Just or Unjust?    68
    Conclusions                               85

**3. Administrative Compensation:**
**Brave New World?**                                              **88**
    Identifying 'Compensation'                88
    Accident Compensation                     91
    Compensation as Good Administration       105
    Damages, Human Rights, and Compensation   109
    Towards a General Principle?              116

**General Conclusion: Collective Consumption
Reinstated** 124

**Annex: State Liability and French
Administrative Law** 134

Index 142

# Table of Cases

A and others *v.* The National Blood Authority [2001]
3 All ER 289 ........................................... 35
AB *v.* South West Water Services [1993] 1 All
ER 609 ................................................ 51
'Agent Orange' Product Liability Litigation, In re 100
FRD 718 (EDNY 1983), affirmed 81 F 2d 145
(2d circuit 1987) ...................................... 46
Ahearn *v.* Fibreboard Corporation 162 FRD 505
(ED Tex 1995) ........................................ 48
Akenzua *v.* Home Secretary (2002) ECWA Civ 470 .... 131
Aksoy *v.* Turkey [1996] 23 EHRR 553.................... 71
Alcock *v.* Chief Constable of S. Yorkshire Police
[1991] 3 WLR 1057 .................................... 50
Alden *v.* Maine 527 US 706 (1999) ...................... 63
Alexandrou *v.* Oxford [1993] 4 All ER 328.............. 73
Anns *v.* Merton London Borough Council [1978]
AC 728............................................ 18, 37
Anufrijeva *v.* Southwark LBC [2003] EWCA
Civ 406....................................... 113-15, 118
Arizona Tobacco Products, CE 28 Feb 1992 [1992]
Rec 78............................................. 52, 60
Ashby *v.* White (1703) 14 St. Tr. 695 .................... 130
Ashingdane *v.* United Kingdom (1985) 7 EHRR 528 .... 74
Aydin *v.* Turkey (1998) 25 EHRR 251.................... 77
Barrett *v.* Enfield LBC [1999] 3 WLR 79............... 29, 73
BAT *v.* Cowell (2002) VSCA 197 ........................ 53
Bernard *v.* Enfield LBC [2001] EWCA Civ 2717 ........ 112
Biret International SA *v.* Council, Case T-174/01
[2002] ECR II-17...................................... 66
Biret International SA *v.* Council, Case C-93/02P ....... 66
Etablissements Biret et Cie SA *v.* Council, Case
C-94/02 P, Opinion of A-G Alber, 15 May 2003
Judgment of 30 September 2003 ...................... 66

Bivens *v.* Six Unknown Named Agents of the Federal
    Bureau of Narcotics 403 US 388 (1971)............ 24, 80
Blanco TC 8 February 1873, Rec 1er supplement 61 .... 135
Botrill *v.* A [2001] 3 NZLR 622 (NZ CA); [2003]
    1 AC 449 ............................................. 131-2
Brinckmann Tabkfabriken *v.* Skatteministeriet, Case
    C-319/96 [1998] ECR I-5255 ........................... 52
Burmah Oil *v.* Lord Advocate [1965] AC 75 ............. 24
Burnie Port Authority *v.* General Jones Pty Ltd
    (1994) 179 CLR 520 .................................... 18
Caparo Industries plc *v.* Dickman [1990] 1 All ER
    568.................................................. 18, 73
Capital & Counties plc *v.* Hampshire County
    Council [1997] 2 All ER 865 ......................... 139
Cattanach *v.* Melchior [2003] HCA 38 (16 July 2003) ... 139
Chorzow case (1928) PCIJ Ser A, no 17, at 29 ........... 54
City of Kamloops *v.* Nielsen [1984] 2 SCR 2 ............. 18
Clubb *v.* Saanich (District) (1996) 46 LR 4th 253 ......... 78
Cocks *v.* Thanet RDC [1983] 2 AC 286 ................. 119
Commission *v.* France, Commission *v.* Greece,
    González Sánchez *v.* Medicina Asturiana Cases
    C-52/00, C-154/00, C-193/00 [2002] ELR I-3827...... 140
Commission *v.* Greece, Case C-45/91 [1992] ECR
    I-2509................................................. 64
Commission *v.* Greece, Case C-387/97 [2000] ECR
    I-5047................................................. 64
Commission *v.* Spain, Case C-278/01 (judgment of
    25 November 2003) .................................... 65
Commune de Hannapes, CE 29 April 1998, RDP 1998.
    1012 ................................................. 139
Connaughton *v.* Council, Case T-541/193 [1997]
    ECR II-549............................................. 67
Consorts N'Guyen, Joaun, Consorts Pavan, CE 26
    May 1995 (Ass) RFDA 1995.748 ...................... 140
Cooper *v.* Wandsworth Board of Works (1863) 14
    CBNS 180 ............................................. 22
Couitéas, CE 30 November 1923, Rec 789 ................ 60
Crimmins *v.* Stevedoring Committee (1999) 200
    CLR 1 ................................................. 37

Dangeville, CAA Paris 1 July 1992 [1992] Rec 558; CE
(Ass) 30 Oct 1996 [1996] Rec 399...................... 60
De Wilde, Ooms and Versyp *v.* Belgium (No 2)
(1972) 1 EHRR 438 .................................. 69
Deep Vein Thrombosis, In Re [2003] 3 WLR 961 ........ 45
Denmark *v.* Turkey, Application No 34383/97
(judgment of 5 April 2000)........................... 70
Dixon *v.* Metropolitan Board of Works (1881) 7 QBD
418..................................................... 31
Doe *v.* Metropolitan Toronto Board of Commissioners
of Police .........................................27, 77, 112
Donoghue *v.* Folkestone Properties Ltd [2003] 2 WLR
1138................................................. 11, 128
Donoghue *v.* Stevenson [1932] AC 562.................. 15
Dunlop *v.* Woollahra Municipal Council [1981]
2 WLR 693............................................. 117
East Suffolk Catchment Board *v.* Kent [1941] AC 74 .... 37
Entick *v.* Carrington (1765) 2 Wils. KB 275 ......... 23, 135
Fairchild *v.* Newhaven Funeral Services Ltd [2002]
UKHL 22; [2002] 3 WLR 89 ........................... 14
Florida Prepaid Postsecondary Education Expense
Board *v.* College Savings Bank 527 US 627 (1999);
College Savings Bank *v.* Florida Prepaid
Postsecondary Education Expense Board 527
US 666 (1999).......................................... 63
Francovich and Bonafaci *v.* Italy, Joined Cases
6, 9/90 [1991] ECR I-5357 ........................ 56, 118
Frost *v.* Chief Constable of S. Yorkshire Police [1998]
3 WLR 1758........................................... 50
Georgine *v.* Amchem Products Inc 157 FRD 246
(ED Pa 1994)........................................... 48
Germany *v.* European Parliament and Commission,
Case C-376/198 [2000] ECR I-8419 ................... 52
Glossop *v.* Heston and Isleworth Local Board (1879)
12 Ch. D. 102 ........................................ 32
Goldman *v.* Hargrave [1967] AC 645 ................... 11
Governor Wall's Case (1802) 28 St. Tr. 51............... 23
Hartmann *v.* Council and Commission, Case
T-2094 [1997] ECR II-595............................. 67

Hedley Byrne *v.* Heller [1964] AC 465................... 18
Heil *v.* Rankin [2000] 2 WLR 1173...................... 104
Herrington *v.* British Railways Board [1972]
  AC 877 .......................................... 11, 34
Hill *v.* Chief Constable of Yorkshire [1988] 2 All ER
  238............................................. 29, 73, 78
Home Office *v.* Dorset Yacht Co. Ltd. [1970] 2
  WLR 1140 ................................. 17-19, 37, 129
James *v.* United Kingdom (1986) 8 EHRR 123 ........... 73
JD and others *v.* East Berkshire Community Health
  Trust and others [2003] EWCA Civ 1151 .......... 29, 84
John Munroe (Acrylics) Ltd *v.* London Fire and Civil
  Defence Authority [1996] 3 WLR 988 ................ 139
Jolley *v.* Sutton LBC [2000] 1 WLR 1082............. 21, 128
Junior Books *v.* Veitchi [1983] 1 AC 523................. 17
Kampffmeyer *v.* Commission, Joined Cases 5,7,
  13-24/66 [1967] ECR 245 ............................ 60
Kechichin, CE 30 Nov 2001 AJDA 2002.133............. 139
Kent *v.* Griffiths [2000] 2 All ER 474................... 73
Kirkham *v.* Chief Constable of Manchester [1989] 2
  QB 283 ............................................ 73
Knightley *v.* Johns [1982] 1 All ER 301 ................. 73
Könle *v.* Republic of Austria, Case C-302/97 [1999]
  ECR I-3099 ........................................ 63
Kuddus *v.* Chief Constable of Leicestershire
  Constabulary [2001] 2 WLR 1789................... 130-1
Laboratoires Pharmaceutiques Bergaderm and
  Goupil *v.* Commission, Case C-352/98 P [2000]
  ECR I-5291 ........................................ 67
Lagrand (Germany *v.* USA), judgment of 27
  June 2001............................................ 55
Leach *v.* Money (1765) 19 St. Tr. 1001 ............... 23, 135
Leakey *v.* National Trust [1980] 1 All ER 17 ............ 34
Leander *v.* Sweden (1987) 9 EHRR 433.................. 122
Lister *v.* Hesely HA [2001] 2 WLR 1311 ............. 84, 130
Marc Rich & Co *v.* Bishop Rock Marine Co Ltd
  [1996] AC 211 .................................... 36, 108
Marcic *v.* Thames Water Utilities Ltd [2002] QB
  929 (CA); [2003] 3 WLR 1603 (HL) ................. 31-5

Marcic *v.* Thames Water (No 2) [2002] QB 1003 ......... 31
Mostyn *v.* Fabrigas (1774) 1 Cowp. 161 .................. 23
Mulder I, Case 120/86 [1988] ECR ....................... 67
Mulder II, Case C-104/89 [1992] ECR I-3061 ............ 67
Musgrave *v.* Pulido (1879) 5 App Cas 102 .............. 23
Northern Sandblasting Pty Ltd *v.* Harris (1997) 146
    ALR 572 ................................................ 21
O'Reilly *v.* Mackman [1983] 2 AC 237 .................. 119
O'Rourke *v.* Camden LBC [1997] 3 WLR 86 ......... 118-19
Osman *v.* Ferguson and another [1993] 4 All
    ER 344 ................................................. 72
Osman *v.* United Kingdom (1998) 29
    EHRR 245. ................................... 29, 71-5, 125
Overseas Tankship (UK) *v.* Morts Dock and
    Engineering Co. (The Wagon Mound No. 1)
    [1961] AC 388 ......................................... 19
Overseas Tankship (UK) *v.* Miller Steamship
    Property Co. (The Wagon Mound No. 2) [1967] 1
    AC 611. ................................................ 19
Perre *v.* Apand Pty Ltd (1999) 198 CLR 180 ............. 18
Perruche, Cass Civ, Ass Plen 17 Nov 2000, D.2001
    Juris 332 .............................................. 139
Phelps *v.* Hillingdon LBC [2000] 3 WLR 776 ....... 29, 120
Philips *v.* Eyre (1867) LR 4 QB 225. ..................... 23
Powell and Rayner *v.* United Kingdom (1989) 12
    EHRR 287. .............................................. 74
Pyrenees Council *v.* Day (1998) 192 CLR 330 ............ 18
R *v.* Chief Constable of N Wales ex p AB (1998) 3
    WLR ........................................... 27, 57, 78
R *v.* Criminal Injuries Compensation Board
    ex p Lain [1967] 2 QB 864. ............................ 94
R *v.* Dytham (1979) 2 QB 722. .......................... 131
R *v.* McGillivray (1990) 56 CCC (3d) 304 ............... 79
R *v.* North and East Devon Health Authority ex p
    Coughlan [2000] 2 WLR 622 .......................... 115
R *v.* Secretary of State for Transport ex p Factortame
    (No 2), Case C-213/89 [1990] ECR I-2433 ............. 62
R *v.* Secretary of State for Transport ex p Factortame
    (No 3) [1992] 3 WLR 288. ............................. 62

R *v.* Secretary of State for Transport ex p Factortame
(No 5) (1999) 3 WLR 1062 ............................ 65
R (Bernard) *v.* Enfield LBC [2002] EWHC
2282 .............................................. 112, 120
R (Cowl) *v.* Plymouth City Council
(Practice Note) [2002] 1 WLR 803 .................... 115
R (KB and others) *v.* Mental Health Review Tribunal
and Health Secretary [2003] EWHC 193 .............. 112
Reeman *v.* Department of Transport and Others
[1997] 2 Lloyds Rep 648 ............................. 108
Rees *v.* Darlington Memorial Hospital NHS Trust
(2003) 3 WLR 1091 .................................... 139
Regnault-Desrozier, CE 28 March 1919, S 1918.
III. 25 ................................................ 138
Robinson *v.* Workington Corporation (1897)
1 QB 619. ............................................. 31
Romeo *v.* Conservation Commission of the Northern
Territory (1998) 151 ALR 263. ..................... 20, 128
Roncarelli *v.* Duplessis (1959) 16 DLR (2d) 689 ......... 130
Rookes *v.* Barnard [1964] AC 1129. ...................... 24
Rudolph Wolff & Co Ltd and Noranda Inc. *v.* The
Crown [1990] 1 SCR 695, 69 DLR (4th) 392 ............ 38
S, W (Children) Re, (Care Order. Implementation
Care Plan) [2002] 2 WLR 720 ....................... 81-2
Saint and Murray *v.* Council and Commission, Case
T-554/93 [1997] ECR II-563. ........................... 67
Seminole Tribe *v.* Florida 517 US 44 (1996). .............. 63
Simpson *v.* AG (Baigent's case) [1994] 3 NZLR 667 ...... 80
Smeaton *v.* Ilford Corporation [1954] Ch 450 ............ 31
Smith *v.* Eric Bush, Harris *v.* Wyre Forest District
Council [1995] 1 AC 831 .............................. 108
Smith *v.* Littlewoods Organisation Ltd. [1987]
AC 241 ................................................ 19
State of New South Wales *v.* Ryan and Graham
Barclay Oyster Properties Ltd (2002) HCA 54 ..... 17, 20
Sté Anonyme des Produits Laitiers 'La Fleurette',
CE (Ass) 14 January 1938 Rec 25 ...................... 60
Stovin *v.* Wise (Norfolk CC, third party) [1996] 3
WLR 388 .............................................. 38

Strettons Derby Brewers *v.* Derby Corporation (1894)
1 Ch 431 ............................................. 31
Stubbings and others *v.* United Kingdom (1996) 23
EHRR 213............................................ 74
Sutherland Shire Council *v.* Heyman (1985) 157 CLR
424 .................................................. 18
Swinney *v.* CC of Northumbria Police Force [1996] 3
WLR 968............................................. 73
Thompson *v.* Commissioner of Metropolitan Police
[1998] QB 498................................... 24, 104
Three Rivers District Council *v.* Governor and Company
of the Bank of England [1996] 3 All ER 558; [2000]
2 WLR 1220.............................. 36, 130, 139
Tomlinson *v.* Congleton Borough Council [2003]
2 WLR 1120...................................... 11, 128
Trotman *v.* N Yorkhire CC [1999] LGR 584......... 84, 130
U (A Child), B (A Child) (Serious Injury Standard
of Proof) [2004] EWCA Civ 567....................... 29
US *v.* Philip Morris and BAT (Investments) 2003
EWCA Civ 3028...................................... 53
US *v.* Philip Morris Inc 116 F Supp 2d 131(DDC 2000),
156 F Supp 2d 1 (DDC 2001)......................... 52
Van Oppen *v.* Clerk to the Bedford Charity Referees
[1990] 1 WLR 235.................................... 129
Von Deetzen, Case 170/86 [1988] ECR 2355............. 67
Vowles *v.* Evans [2003] 1 WLR 1607 ................... 129
W and D *v.* Meah [1986] 1 All ER 935 ................. 102
Watson *v.* British Board of Boxing Control [2001]
2 WLR 1256...................................... 36, 129
Wells *v.* Wells [1999] 1 AC 345........................ 104
Wilkes *v.* Wood (1763) 2 Wils. KB 203 .............. 23, 135
X *v.* United Kingdom, App. no 7154/75, 14 DR 31
(1978) ......................................... 86, 125
X (Minors) *v.* BedfordshireCC, M *v.* Newham LBC
[1995] 2 AC 633 ......................... 23, 27, 80, 81
Z and others *v.* United Kingdom (2001) 34 EHRR
97 ............................................. 75-7, 125
Zuckerfabrik Schöppenstedt *v.* Council, Case
5/71 [1971] ECR 975 ................................ 58

# Introduction:
# Problem without Solution?

In 1995, when last I undertook to write about state liability, I called my contribution 'problem without solution'.[1] This was no doubt a pointer to my unsettled state of mind. It must be said, however, that, with the brave exception of David Cohen,[2] no other contributor to the colloquium at which my pessimistic paper was presented showed any great willingness to propound a comprehensive theory of state liability. I cannot say that the considerable intellectual energy spent nearly ten years later in researching these Clarendon lectures has brought me any nearer to a coherent theory. This may be partly symptomatic of the pragmatic approach of common lawyers to legal problems and of the approach to state liability in the common law world. Paradoxically, indeed, the subject of these lectures is a non-subject for common lawyers. We prefer to talk of the liability of public authorities and of the Crown. But I chose the title of these lectures with great deliberation. The term 'state', in contrast to the familiar terminology of Crown and public authorities, possesses no technical, legal resonance for tort lawyers and carries little intellectual baggage, at least inside the domestic legal system.

On reflection, the malaise that caused me to draw back from the problems of state liability was emotional as well as intellectual. We were living through a period when

---

[1] C. Harlow, 'State Liability: Problem Without Solution' (1995) 6 *NJCL* 67. The paper is published with the other contributions to the colloquium, called by the Canadian Government with a view to reform of Crown liability in Canada, in a special issue of the *National Journal of Constitutional Law*.

[2] D. Cohen, 'Responding to Government Failure' (1995) 6 *NJCL* 23.

attitudes to the state were changing rapidly. In the welfare state, distributive justice, in the broad sense of fairer and more equal distribution of resources, had been an acceptable collective goal. It formed a background against which state accident compensation could be just another public service, aimed at keeping accident victims outside the safety net of national assistance. Accident compensation plans, widely discussed by academics, were not beyond the bounds of political possibility, even if no such plan actually made it to the policy agenda of a British government. But as I wrote, the era of 'cradle to grave' welfare, when medical services, education, and social assistance were seen as integral ingredients of the comprehensive Beveridge policy of social progress,[3] was largely over. The state was, at least notionally, being rolled back. The days of a state that intervened directly in the market to direct the economy, and in which major utilities were in public ownership, were numbered. Publicly owned services were being broken up one by one; privatization and contracting out were the new order of the day. The tide had turned against distributive justice.

Distributive justice is a term often used loosely by lawyers to draw a line between those sorts of income redistribution that they see as properly the subject of tort law and those they think should be left for political action. As the term will recur throughout these lectures, it is important to clarify at this early stage in what sense it is being used. Obviously, distributive justice implies some sort of *distribution*, usually of resources. To Ishtak Englard, distributive justice is 'directed at distributing a given object among persons according to a criterion of merit',[4] to Sir Robert Carnwarth it means simply a 'sharing of the cake'.[5] In

---

[3] *Social Insurance and the Social Services*, Cmnd 6404 (1942) (The Beveridge Report).

[4] I. Englard, *The Philosophy of Tort Law* (London: Dartmouth, 1993) at 11. Arguably, merit is immaterial; distributive justice is often aimed specifically at the underprivileged, irrespective of merit.

[5] R. Carnwarth, 'The Liability of Public Authorities in Tort—Corrective and Distributive Justice' (unpublished paper).

both cases, attention centres on the cake and cake-eaters, the conduct of the cake-cutter being immaterial. In this sense, state-funded accident or criminal injuries compensation, not being based on the negligence or legal obligation of the state, fall within the definition of distributive justice. Thus Cohen's 'entitlement theory' of state liability treats compensation as a marginal form of distributive justice, parasitic, as it were, on the wider, resource-sharing distributive principle.[6] In these lectures, the term distributive justice is often used in this loose sense.

Political philosopher Brian Barry draws a rather different line. Barry distinguishes 'distributive' from 'aggregative' political principles according to whether *collective* or *individual* interests are involved.[7] Aggregative principles are those relating to the collective consumption of goods enjoyed by and benefiting the community or a substantial section of the community. Distributive principles, on the other hand, refer to that share of the collective goods that individuals have for themselves. Discussing responsibility in public law, Peter Cane introduces the terminology of 'public' and 'private' to make a similar point. He uses the term 'distributive justice' to describe the balancing of public versus private interests, which he regards as an important public law function:[8]

Public law defines what are public functions for its purposes, and public law principles of responsibility provide an answer to the distributive question of how to balance the public's interest in the promotion of the public good through the performance of public functions, against the interests of citizens in freedom of action, security of person and property, and the promotion of

---

[6] D. Cohen, 'Tort Law and the Crown: Administrative Compensation and the Modern State' in K. Cooper-Stephenson and E. Gibson (eds), *Tort Theory* (York: Captus University Publications, 1993) at 361. The theory is set out and discussed in Lecture 3, below.

[7] B. Barry, *Political Argument* (London: Routledge, 1965) ch. 3. See also D. Miller, *Social Justice* (Oxford: Clarendon, 1976) at 18–20; P. McAuslan, 'Administrative Law, Collective Consumption and Judicial Policy' (1983) 46 *MLR* 1.

[8] P. Cane, *Responsibility in Law and Morality* (Oxford: Hart Publishing, 2002) at 252.

their well-being as individuals or as members of some group within society (as opposed to society as a whole).

Although Cane does not go on to discuss this further, it is undoubtedly widely believed that this type of balancing function is an inherent feature in cases involving the state and public bodies. This is a view that has traditionally attracted the English judiciary. It makes it possible to view public welfare services, such as housing and education, which redistribute resources in the form of tangible benefits as 'aggregative' forms of distributive justice in the sense in which Barry uses the term. Such benefits represent a form of collective consumption designed for the benefit of the community at large and not primarily of individuals, in which case, the notion of distributive justice provides no justification for individual entitlements to compensation.[9] An alternative view held equally strongly is, however, that these questions lie wholly outside the ambit of tort law. Tort law should be objective; it deals purely with relationships of corrective justice and should remain entirely indifferent to issues of social utility or economic efficiency. Whether public or private parties are in question, liability should turn 'on what the defendant has done, rather than on who he is'.[10] This division of opinion lies behind the use made by judges of the public/private distinction in many cases.

Part of the problem that faced me as I wrote in 1995 was that the collective ideal, with which I was broadly speaking comfortable, was suddenly thrown in doubt. The welfare state was shrinking but, I had noticed, belief in distribution had not necessarily withered with it. We were beginning to see the evolution of a 'compensation culture'. Linguistically, privatized public services were being commercialized; they had suddenly acquired 'customers' and 'markets'. 'Citizen's Charters', fashionable as a means of ensuring quality,[11] were little more than disguised 'Public Custom-

---

[9] Further discussed in Lecture 3.

[10] Fletcher, 'Fairness and Utility in Tort Theory' 85 *Harv. LR* 534, 537–8 (1972). The issue is discussed more fully in Lecture 1.

[11] *The Citizen's Charter, Raising the Standard*, Cm 1599 (1991).

ers' Charters', creating pretended 'entitlements' to punctual trains or prompt medical attention. The effect was to encourage the consumer ideology, evident in the rise of consumer protection law, to cross the public/private frontier and seep into the world of public services.

Within the shrinking boundaries of the welfare state, tort law was assuming a 'last ditch function' of filling gaps in declining welfare services. It had become machinery for distributive justice. Tort law was being asked to supply for the few what retreating public services were taking from the many. This was one sense in which it could be termed the 'last outpost of the welfare state'. But, slightly differently, something of a role reversal was taking place, a mood of judicial responsibility to take care of 'vulnerable parties'.[12] As Spigelman CJ put it in Australia:

The idea that governments are in some way responsible for caring for all citizens—as it was put, 'from cradle to grave'—contains a strong element of paternalism that has now been rejected in most advanced industrial countries as the basis of government intervention to attain social policy objectives. An element of welfare state paternalism, driven by the same sense of compassion, is not absent from day to day judicial decision making about when a person ought to receive compensation, even in our fault based system.

The way was opening for an expansive, victim-oriented tort law.

A risk-averse society was being shaped, in which state services were seen as capable of wrapping every citizen in a personal security blanket.[13] Cohen describes a mood of 'generalised reliance', where 'individuals, growing up in the arms of an activist state, ha[d] come to expect, in some unstated perhaps unconscious way, that a paternalistic albeit beneficent state surround[ed] them'.[14] Public actors were asked increasingly to plan for risk, and risk became a

---

[12] J. J. Spigelman, 'Negligence: the Last Outpost of the Welfare State' (2002) 76 *ALJ* 432 also available at www.lawlink.nsw.gov.au/sc

[13] V. Roussel, 'Changing Definitions of Risk and Responsibility in French Political Scandals' (2002) 29 *JLS* 461.

[14] Cohen, above note 2.

benchmark against which all the activities of state and government were to be measured:[15] in well-organized hospitals, accidents should not happen and deaths should not occur; in properly policed streets, crime should be impossible. But just as the flip side of security is police surveillance, so the price paid for a risk-free environment is regulation. The modern state, in which today I sit and write these words, is characterized above all by its regulatory functions. The regulatory state operates on the risk-averse society, where regulation is pervasive and the routine use of the vocabulary and procedural tools for purposes of social control is both accepted and acceptable.[16] Failure to regulate for risk now points to state responsibility, carrying correlative individual entitlements. Distributive justice is slowly extending to security, and security is no longer an aggregative but a distributive good. The 'rights revolution' has built up the compensation culture, an almost inevitable development to which the politicians who 'brought rights home' deliberately closed their eyes. Perhaps they had missed the expansionist mentality of international law and the extent to which the pervasive discourse of human rights was now infused with legalism. Transnational courts succumbed to the prevailing 'I-want-one-too' consumer mentality, rushing to fill their remedial toolkits with shiny, new remedies, a phenomenon that has added considerable momentum to the tort revolution.

State liability remains for me a problem of tort law, for which tort law must provide the conceptual answers. I believe that, in an age of democratic and supposedly accountable government, the Diceyan doctrine of equality before the law[17] needs no defending: its appeal is immediate and instinctive: it conforms to 'a widely-held political ideal'.[18] Equality demands that state liability must

---

[15] Fisher, 'The Rise of the Risk Commonwealth and the Challenge for Administrative Law' [2003] *PL* 455.

[16] R. Baldwin, C. Scott, and C. Hood (eds), 'Introduction', in *A Reader on Regulation* (Oxford: Oxford University Press, 1998) at 2.

[17] A. V. Dicey, *Introduction to the Study of the Law of the Constitution* (10th edn by ECS Wade, London: Macmillan, 1959).

[18] P. Hogg, *Liability of the Crown* (2nd edn, Toronto: Carswell, 1989) at 1.

somehow be assimilated into the ordinary civil law system administered by the 'ordinary courts'; parity means the subjection of the state and its officials to the ordinary principles of civil liability. Those who have sworn allegiance to parity and equality must face the ensuing problems squarely. The case once made for a specialist jurisdiction, capable of devising a specialized public law of liability,[19] is not and never has been a political runner.

What I have to offer in these lectures is an unabashedly functionalist view of what is going on. I understand by functionalism no more than a purposive understanding of law through its operation.[20] I have consciously chosen the terminology of 'functionalism' in preference to that of 'instrumentalism', which to me suggests the deliberate use of law for purposes of social control. The questions functionalists ask about tort law seem to me to be questions of the moment, not only in the sense that they are fashionable but also because they are momentous. Functionalism calls for an audit of the social value and economic effectiveness of tort law; in this, I am content to follow where those masters of tort law, Patrick Atiyah[21] and the late John Fleming,[22] have led. To my mind, they have shown that tort law would fail any rational 'Three Es' audit many times over; it is uneconomic and inefficient, in the sense that the money expended on recovery of damages greatly exceeds the amount of damages recovered, while its effectiveness for either of its key objectives of compensation and deterrence is very dubious indeed.

---

[19] The case was brilliantly advanced by J. Mitchell, 'The Causes and Effects of an Absence of the Absence of a System of Public Law in the United Kingdom' [1965] *PL* 95. My response, to which I broadly hold today, is to be found in C. Harlow, ' "Public" and "Private" Law: Definition Without Distinction' (1980) 43 *MLR* 241 with a riposte from G. Samuel, 'Public and Private Law: A Private Lawyer's Response' (1983) 46 *MLR* 558. Here I have chosen to relegate the question to an Annex (below at 134).

[20] Compare E. Weinrib, *The Idea of Private Law* (Boston, Mass.: Harvard University Press, 1995) at 3.

[21] P. S. Atiyah, *Accidents, Compensation and the Law* (London: Weidenfeld and Nicolson, 1970).

[22] Notably, J. Fleming, *The American Tort Process* (Oxford: Clarendon, 1987).

It may then seem surprising that I have chosen to start my first lecture with a look at tort law's conceptual bases. However, while I believe that, to understand tort law, it is important to pay regard to its objectives; at the same time I accept law's symbolic and standard-setting functions. I therefore subscribe to Jane Stapleton's view that tort law needs to give 'the appearance of being fair, sensible and *focused*'.[23] In my first lecture, I shall argue that the steady, if intermittent, process of expansion at which I have been hinting has landed tort law in a position where it sits uncomfortably within its conceptual framework. But functionalism suggests further and more significant questions. Essentially, as we shall see, the tort action is *individuated*. If, however, tort law is to achieve efficiency and effectiveness as well as fairness, then judges in resolving apparently private disputes need to adopt a wider perspective. This, I shall suggest in the third lecture, they are in fact starting to do, though I shall question the preference for concealing their functionalist reasoning behind the opaque and catchall formalist terminology of 'public interest'.

These lectures argue consistently for the restraint of tort law and for a less profligate use of damages as a remedy. This does not mean, however, that I am deaf to the cries of distributive justice or favour a 'taxpayer's charter' of judicial parsimony. True, I deplore the litigation tactics that have set the state squarely within the sights of lawyers tempted by its apparently bottomless coffers. As I have suggested, I see the ineffectual tort system as a remedy of last resort. But I believe strongly in collective responsibility and social solidarity. I also believe that a measure of compensation, promptly and voluntarily proffered, is an integral element in social solidarity. I see statutory or administrative compensation as offering a viable and often preferable alternative to tort law and a more understanding approach on the part of judges to alternative remedies is undoubtedly necessary. Equally, a more gracious attitude

---

[23] Stapleton, 'In Restraint of Tort' in P. Birks (ed), *The Frontiers of Liability* (Oxford: Oxford University Press, 1994) II at 83 (emphasis mine).

on the part of officialdom would be helpful, while it is high time too for politicians to recognize their responsibilities. These lectures argue for nothing more nor less than a new concordat, in which legislators, judges, policy-makers—and even academics—come together to fashion a new and less aggressive system of state responsibility, founded on values of community and social solidarity. This may mean a re-thinking of traditional beliefs in sanction and deterrence in favour of an alternative vision of justice as primarily re-storative. This is not an easy option and many of my readers will no doubt dismiss it outright as unduly idealistic.

# 1

# Corrective Justice in the Frame

Corrective justice, currently the most fashionable justification of tort law, also correlates most closely with the law of torts as it has emerged historically, a coincidence lending legitimacy to the theory. Weinrib, an extreme proponent of the corrective justice theory, explains the concept as 'the pattern of justificatory coherence latent *in the bipolar private law relationship of the plaintiff to the defendant*'.[1] He claims no particular novelty for this definition of tort law as:

(i) inherently bipolar;
(ii) premised on an inter-personal relationship between two parties; and
(iii) a relationship of right and duty or, as described by earlier writers, 'a regime of correlative rights and duties'.[2]

For Weinrib, the concept of corrective justice is not only normative but also definitive in the sense of being the *sole justification* for tort law. The concern of tort law is simply to be itself, its rules being justifiable on grounds of coherence;[3] in which case, a functionalist might retort, the subject clearly falls far short of Weinrib's expectations. But the retort would fall on deaf ears: Weinrib asserts that

---

[1] E. Weinrib, *The Idea of Private Law* (Boston, Mass.: Harvard University Press, 1995) at 10 (emphasis mine) and 19. Weinrib sees corrective justice as explicatory of all civil liability, though he focuses on tort law.

[2] See H. Street, *Street on Torts* (7th edn, London: Butterworths, 1983) at 3: 'The law of torts is concerned with those situations where the conduct of one party causes or threatens harm to the interests of other parties'. Street is by instinct a functionalist, however, as he remarks that 'the function and purpose of the law of torts' are of 'greater import' than definition.

[3] Weinrib, above note 1, at 3.

functionalism is, despite its current popularity, quite simply 'mistaken'.[4]

It should be borne in mind that Cane firmly denies the possibility of basing an explanatory account of tort law on any single principle or doctrine,[5] a view that I share. At the same time, I share his view of the corrective justice concept as a helpful analytical tool. Cane himself steers clear of a functionalist critique of tort law—of which he is very well capable[6]—in the sense of an appraisal of tort law according to its fitness for purpose.

Weinrib's analysis stresses the *objectivity* of tort law, a point of great significance in the context of these lectures. Weinrib 'posits a bipolar structure of reparation . . . indifferent to matters of status, wealth and merits of the parties. Gains and losses are to be annulled without reference to these considerations'.[7] We should note that this has never been more than a half-truth: damages have often been denied to plaintiffs deemed unworthy,[8] while recent cases have sometimes tailored the duty of care to the resources and circumstances of the defendant.[9] The question of resources is currently emerging as an issue of particular difficulty and unease for the judiciary, especially when the liability of the state is in issue. Nonetheless, we need to bear in mind that corrective justice theory stresses the autonomy of tort law, setting it above practical considerations such as resource-allocation, insurance, or other questions too often allowed to intrude into the apportionment of liability in the polluted atmosphere of the courtroom, while at the same time emphasizing that functionalists can

---

[4] Weinrib, above note 1 at 3

[5] P. Cane, *An Anatomy of Tort Law* (Oxford: Hart Publishing, 1997) at 224.

[6] See P. Cane (ed), *Atiyah's Accidents, Compensation and the Law* (6th edn, London: Butterworths, 1999).

[7] R. Rabin, in a joint book review of Cane and Weinrib, 'Law for Law's Sake' 105 *Yale LJ* 2261, 2264.

[8] Originally under the maxim *ex turpi causa non oritur actio*: now usually illegality: see *Pitts v Hunt* [1990] 3 All ER 344. And see Law Com Consultation Paper No 160, *The Illegality Defence in Tort* (2001).

[9] A trend introduced by *Goldman v Hargrave* [1967] AC 645; *Herrington v British Railways Board* [1972] AC 87.

never accept the irrelevance of tort law's 'indirect extrinsic functions'[10] to the imposition of tortious liability.

Cohen in particular blames the influence of 'conservative Diceyan political ideologies' for the failure of courts to take into account 'the particular economic environment within which public bureaucracies operate'.[11] The debate over resource-allocation, and the extent to which it is proper for judges deciding individual cases to take resources into consideration, is a recurring theme of these lectures, to which we shall return nearly as often as the judges themselves.

The basic exposition of corrective justice is capable of nuance.[12] It is significant that, to some writers, the victim's right to compensation is dependent on the wrongful *conduct* of the defendant, an emphasis that justifies restraint and familiar control devices, such as the common law emphasis on causation or awkward bright-lines between act and omission or misfeasance and non-feasance, variations on a common theme and again the occasion of much agonizing by the judiciary in cases involving public authorities. An alternative formulation, according to which 'corrective justice connotes a system of rights and duties that are correlative between identified persons and stem solely *from a particular event*',[13] positions the thorny subject of causation centrally at the forefront of the liability picture.

Other exponents of the corrective justice model of tort law prefer to focus on the *loss* suffered by the plaintiff, suggesting that tort law can, or perhaps should, spring into action whenever a wrongful loss has been suffered.[14] With loss as the starting-point, the outreach of tort law can

[10] Cane, above note 5, at 226–31.

[11] Cohen, 'Tort Law and the Crown: Administrative Compensation and the Modern State' in K. Cooper-Stephenson and E. Gibson (eds), *Tort Theory* (York: Captus University Publications, 1993) at 361.

[12] See S. Perry, 'Loss, Agency, and Responsibility for Outcomes: Three Conceptions of Corrective Justice' in ibid., at 24.

[13] A. Morris, 'On the Normative Foundations of Indirect Discrimination Law: Understanding the Competing Models of Discrimination Law as Aristotelian Forms of Justice' (1995) 15 *OJLS* 199, 205.

[14] J. Coleman, 'Tort Law and the Demands of Corrective Justice' (1992) 67 *Indiana LJ* 349.

be extended on to the terrain of distributive justice, the change of focus breaking the connective link between subject and actor. Reparation can then cease to be the sole responsibility of the wrongdoer and become a shared or community responsibility. This need not necessarily be implemented through the tort system but through a compensation regime or compulsory no-fault insurance plan.[15] But the qualifying adjective 'wrongful' indicates a significant limitation on the field of tort law, in theory, if not always in practice. By tying recompense into the ethical, corrective justice framework of tort law, the adjective points to a balancing process, in which the interests of plaintiff and defendant have to be weighed. The emphasis on *loss* also highlights tort law's compensatory function, marking a step towards today's victim-oriented case law, in which the elastic elements of fault and foreseeability are stretched almost to vanishing point. We can see this in the gradual erosion of the consent defence in negligence cases, which has allowed claimants to recover even when their own conduct seems foolhardy, as when a swimmer takes a headlong dive into unfamiliar waters;[16] we can see it too in the indefinite and often implausible prolongation of chains of causation.[17] These are both typical aspects of the modern law of negligence, beginning to cause particular problems for public authorities engaged in the exercise of supervisory and regulatory functions, to which I shall return at a later stage in this lecture.

Unlike Atiyah's robust functionalist critique of tort law as ineffective and uneconomic machinery for the delivery of accident compensation,[18] corrective justice implies a moral dimension. Cane indeed explicitly justifies his

---

[15] S. Perry, 'Loss, Agency, and Responsibility for Outcomes: Three Conceptions of Corrective Justice', in Cooper-Stephenson and Gibson, above note 11, at 24–7.

[16] Cane, *Anatomy*, above note 5, at 121–2. But see *Tomlinson v Congleton Borough Council* [2003] 2 WLR 1120; *Donoghue v Folkestone Properties Ltd* [2003] 2 WLR 1138 (further discussed below).

[17] *State of New South Wales v Ryan* [2002] HCA 54, discussed below at note 44.

[18] Above note 6. See also *The Damages Lottery* (Oxford: Hart Publishing, 1997).

reclassification of tort law in terms of corrective justice on the ground of the need to reinstate tort law's moral dimension.[19] Weinrib's ivory tower approach, on the other hand, according to which the purpose of tort law is simply to be tort law,[20] enables him to avoid subsidiary questions as to whether the main aim of tort law is compensation or deterrence, which open the door to functionalist evaluations of fitness for purpose.[21] This masks the fact that, inside the corrective justice model of tort law, the two objectives of compensation and deterrence sit uncomfortably and may come into open conflict. In the next section, I shall discuss the expansive trend of tort law in recent years, motored by a concern for compensation. I then turn to the deterrent and sometimes punitive attitude to tort law that permeates the main public law theories of state liability. This point is underscored in my second lecture, when the continental public law tradition is introduced.

### COMPENSATION: TOWARDS A TORT TAX?

The overall objective of tort law, Lord Bingham said recently, 'is to define cases in which the law may *justly* hold one party liable to compensate another'.[22] There would undoubtedly be much judicial and popular support for this assertion. But note the qualifying adverb, which sets a classical boundary. Even if judges throughout the common law world have in recent years leant by and large towards compensation as tort law's primary objective, they recognize the restraints imposed by the corset of corrective justice. This makes it hard to move in other than ambivalent fashion towards the deceptively simple goal. The changed

---

[19] On which Cane feels strongly: see P. Cane, *Responsibility in Law and Morality* (Oxford: Hart Publishing, 2002).

[20] Weinrib, above note 1, at 3.

[21] Weinrib, 'Understanding Tort Law' (1989) 23 *Valparaiso University Law Review* 485, 492.

[22] *Fairchild v Newhaven Funeral Services Ltd* [2002] UKHL 22; [2002] 3 WLR 89 at para 9 (emphasis mine).

judicial attitude to 'victims' and aspiration to protect 'vulnerable parties' have led nonetheless to pressure on the traditional boundaries of tort law. This has been a widespread phenomenon, noted especially by American commentators. Thus Schwartz labels the 1960s and 1970s in the United States, an era in which strict products liability was being forged, a decade of 'plaintiffs greatest hits'. Creativity extended to the 1980s, since when, he thinks, 'courts have rejected invitations to endorse new innovations in liability; moreover they have placed a somewhat conservative gloss on innovations undertaken in previous years'.[23] Huber, who blames the influence of Posner and Calabresi for landing the costs of accidents on producers,[24] talks in polemical language of an 'omnipresent tort tax'. This was:[25]

conceived in the 1950s and set in place in the 1960s and 1970s by a new generation of lawyers and judges. In the space of 20 years they transformed the legal landscape, proclaiming sweeping new rights to sue. . . . But the revolution they made could never have taken place had it not had a component of idealism as well. Tort law, it is widely and passionately believed, is a public-spirited undertaking designed for the protection of the ordinary consumer and worker, the hapless accident victim, the 'little guy'.

Reflecting from across the Atlantic on a 'not so golden' anniversary, Smith and Burns attribute the relentless progress of modern tort law directly to Lord Atkin's formulation of the 'neighbour principle' in the seminal case of *Donoghue v Stevenson*.[26] This, the authors argue, provided a lever to reverse the burden of proof in negligence so that, once the plaintiff has shown a careless causing of harm, the defendant is more likely than not to have to pay damages,

---

[23] G. Schwartz, 'The Beginning and the Possible End of the Rise of Modern American Tort Law' 26 *Georgia L Rev*. 601, 603 (1992).

[24] R. Posner, *Economic Analysis of Law* (Boston, Mass.: Little Brown, 1973, now 5th edn, 1998); G. Calabresi, *The Cost of Accidents* (New Haven, Conn.: Yale University Press, 1970).

[25] P. Huber, *Liability, the Legal Revolution and its Consequences* (New York: Basic Books, 1988) at 4.

[26] *Donoghue v Stevenson* [1932] AC 52.

unless he can show that his situation falls under one of the exceptions where the law of negligence does not apply.[27] After listing several of the exceptions or immunities, many at the time under threat and several of which have now fallen, the authors turn their attention to discussion of the difference between acts and omissions to act as a ground for liability. They see a generalized principle of duty to take care in acting so as to avoid causing harm to others as justifiable; on the other hand, a workable general principle to cover non-feasance or omission to act entails the unacceptable proposition that '[e]veryone is under an obligation to take positive action to prevent harm from happening to others'.[28] But this proposition, derided by Smith and Burns as patently ridiculous, does reflect the assumption of our risk-averse society that public actors are obliged to plan and regulate against risk.[29] It is thus both foreseeable and significant that many of the most difficult cases facing our courts today should concern liability for failure to take preventive action (omission to act) or, where public authorities are concerned, failure to exercise the plenitude of their statutory powers.

Querying the way in which negligence principles are 'worked through' and applied in novel areas, Stapleton criticizes many of the modern developments. She instances: the tendency to base liability on failure by one party to 'control' another; changed attitudes to liability for omissions; a new attitude to the responsibilities of property owners, extending both the ambit and scope of the duties owed; a judicial propensity to impose liability for failure to warn of risks, sometimes even when these are blindingly obvious; and the growing practice of allowing 'leapfrogging' of intermediary parties. The 'leapfrogging' metaphor is used by Stapleton to refer to important changes in the relationship between tort and contract, leading towards the

---

[27] J. C. Smith and P. Burns, 'Donoghue v. Stevenson—the Not So Golden Anniversary' (1983) 46 MLR 147, 150.

[28] At 158.

[29] Introduction, text at note 13.

abolition of privity;[30] I shall, however, use the term more generally, as indicative of a trend to transfer liability from primary to secondary actors, associated with changes in the law of vicarious liability; the conflation of the employer's primary and secondary liability; and imposition of non-delegable duties of care on corporate bodies and public authorities.[31] To these cogent points made by Stapleton should be added the trend to anonymize and institutional-ize tort law by the targeting of negligent *systems* rather than *persons*. These trends have in common that they 'deflect attention away from the party or parties directly and prin-cipally responsible for the damage',[32] with the consequence that the element of fault and blame in the corrective justice paradigm eventually comes to be discounted.

Let us now step back in time to consider a second 'not so golden' anniversary: the *Dorset Yacht* case,[33] where the Home Office was famously held potentially liable for damage to a yacht owned by the Dorset Yacht Company, commandeered by Borstal boys camping on an island in Poole harbour and used by them to escape. I would call this the most significant state liability case of my career, setting the scene for a liability revolution as great as, if not greater than, that usually attributed to *Donoghue v Stevenson*,[34] its expansive potential heightened by the fact that the subject-matter was damage to property occasioning economic loss. (The sole issue in the case, though not reflected in the

---

[30] See *Junior Books v Veitchi* [1983] 1 AC 523, a troublesome case discussed by P. Cane, *Tort Law and Economic Interests* (Oxford: Clarendon, 1991) at 232–4. And see S. Whittaker, 'Privity of Contract and the Tort of Negligence: Future Directions' (1996) 16 *OJLS* 191; J. Adams and R. Brownsword, 'Privity and the Concept of a Network Contract' (1990) 10 *Legal Studies* 12.

[31] A trend identified by E. McKendrick, 'Vicarious Liability and Inde-pendent Contractors—A Re-examination' (1990) 53 *MLR* 770.

[32] J. Stapleton, 'Duty of Care: Peripheral Parties and Alternative Op-portunities for Deterrence' (1995) 111 *LQR* 301, 312.

[33] *Home Office v Dorset Yacht Co. Ltd.* [1970] 2 WLR 1140. For my views at the time see C. Harlow, *Compensation and Government Torts* (London: Sweet and Maxwell, 1982) at 56–7.

[34] Though, Rubinstein, 'Liability in Tort of Judicial Officers' (1964) 15 *UTLJ* 317, 329, attributes the doubtful honour to *Hedley Byrne v Heller* [1964] AC 465, which rendered 'bureaucratic negligence' actionable.

judgment, was whether the taxpayer should foot the bill for a loss underwritten by the plaintiff's insurers, since the Home Office operates a voluntary compensation plan in cases of loss or damage to property caused by absconders from prison, wherever the damage occurs in the immediate neighbourhood of the prison and is not covered by insurance.[35]) Nearly all of Stapleton's expansive factors are present in the *Dorset Yacht* case: the fluid notion of 'control', especially perilous for public authorities, which, unlike private actors, possess so many statutory powers to control third parties; the move from positive acts of wrongdoing towards failure to take appropriate action, opening the possibility of the wide liability for omissions deplored by Smith and Burns; and the transfer of liability from primary wrongdoers (the escapees) to a peripheral party (the state).

Nevertheless, *Dorset Yacht* installed Lord Atkin's formulation of the 'neighbour principle' in *Donoghue v Stevenson* as the 'general principle of civil liability' which, according to Lord Reid, was to be treated as applicable unless there was some justification or valid explanation for its exclusion.[36] As already stated, the effect was to reverse the liability presumption, a change spelled out explicitly in the later case of *Anns v Merton LBC*.[37] The 'two-stage test' installed by this unsatisfactory case enjoins the judge in cases of negligence to ask, once proximity and foreseeability have been established, whether there is any policy reason *against* the imposition of liability? The utility of duty of care as a

---

[35] See Report of the PCA, HC 42 (1973/4) at 112, reprinted in C. Harlow and R. W. Rawlings, *Law and Administration* (London: Weidenfeld and Nicolson, 1984) at 409–10.

[36] [1970] 2 WLR 1140, 1146.

[37] *Anns v Merton London Borough Council* [1978] AC 728. For the status of the test today see *Caparo Industries plc v Dickman* [1990] 1 All ER 568. Compare *Sutherland Shire Council v Heyman* (1985) 157 CLR 424; *Burnie Port Authority v General Jones Pty Ltd* (1994) 179 CLR 520; *Pyrenees Council v Day* (1998) 192 CLR 330 at 409; and *Perre v Apand Pty Ltd* (1999) 198 CLR 180. For Canada, see *City of Kamloops v Nielsen* [1984] 2 SCR 2. And see Neyers, 'Distilling Duty: The Supreme Court of Canada Amends *Anns*' (2002) 118 LQR 221.

control device had virtually been eliminated. As Lord Goff remarked in *Smith v Littlewoods*,[38] one of the few cases directly to invoke *Dorset Yacht*, its function had now become 'not so much to identify cases where liability is imposed as to identify those where it is not'. Read in the context of liability for all *foreseeable* damage set in place by the *Wagon Mound* cases[39] and the subsequent opening of the tort system to cases of economic loss,[40] the scene was set for wide and rapid expansion. Reflecting a public expectation that those who suffered loss ('victims') should almost automatically recover damages, lawyers became 'adept at devising technical devices to achieve this'.[41] The same could be said of many judges. So we find Lord Cooke, reflecting on the recovery of 'pure' economic loss in negligence, arguing that 'no inexorable logic compels the conclusion that a defect in quality is not redressible in negligence'.[42] But does any 'inexorable logic' suggest the contrary?

In *Dorset Yacht*, Lord Reid had treated the familiar floodgates argument, together with the potential of liability decisions for a 'chilling effect' on public policy-making to the withering comment, 'Her Majesty's civil servants are made of sterner stuff'! The floodgates, were, however soon to open.[43]

The legal profession, increasingly engaged in the respectable activity of allocation of losses to pockets other than those of its own

---

[38] *Smith v Littlewoods Organisation Ltd.* [1987] AC 241, 280.

[39] *Overseas Tankship (UK) v Morts Dock and Engineering Co. (The Wagon Mound No. 1)* [1961] AC 388; *Overseas Tankship (UK) v Miller Steamship Property Co. (The Wagon Mound No. 2)* [1967] 1 AC 611. And see Davies, 'The Road from Morocco: Polemis Through Donoghue to No Fault' (1981) 45 *MLR* 534; Kidner, 'Remoteness of Damage: The Duty-interest Theory and the Re-interpretaion of the Wagon Mound' (1989) 9 *Legal Studies* 1.

[40] See further P. Cane, *Tort Law and Economic Interests* (Oxford: Oxford University Press, 1991); B. Feldthusen, 'The Recovery of Pure Economic Loss in Canda: Proximity, Justice, Rationality and Chaos' (1996) 24 *Manitoba LJ* 1; B. Feldthusen, *Economic Negligence: The Recovery of Pure Economic Loss* (2nd edn, Toronto: Carswell, 1989).

[41] Stapleton, above note 32, at 302.

[42] Sir Robin Cooke, 'The Condition of the Law of Tort' in P. Birks (ed), *The Frontiers of Liability* (Oxford: Oxford University Press, 1994) II at 51.

[43] Harlow, above note 33, at 49–50.

clients has amply compensated for any earlier lack of enterprise. The 'deep pockets' of government and local authorities supplied from the apparently endless resources of the tax and rate funds have, as speakers in the debate on the Crown Proceedings Bill realized they might, proved an irresistible temptation to litigants. . . . The categories of negligence are truly never closed and public authorities are learning this to their (or our) cost.

What, I wonder, would Lord Reid have made of the recent Australian case of *State of New South Wales v Ryan*,[44] where the plaintiff became ill after eating oysters polluted with a hepatitis virus, given to him by a relative who had purchased them from a private commercial oyster-grower? Shades of *Donoghue v Stevenson*? But the oysters had been farmed in a lake owned by the State of New South Wales, which also possessed powers, albeit limited, to control and regulate the oyster industry. The Great Lakes Council, a public authority with broad responsibility for pollution and environmental matters, was also in the picture, while the state was represented on the Management Committee and had powers to prohibit the taking of oysters from the lake. 'Leapfrogging' claims were consequently made against both peripheral parties, the claims being based on failure to exercise their statutory powers. Without the *Dorset Yacht* case, could this litigation have been contemplated, let alone have engaged the attention of five very senior judges in the High Court of Australia?

Again, take the case of *Romeo v Conservation Commission of the Northern Territory*,[45] where a young woman, messing about in a public car park, was seriously injured by a fall from cliffs. A thin case, which ultimately failed to convince a distinguished bench of High Court judges, was made against the Conservation Commission, in charge of the beauty spot where the car park was located. The case was based on the ground of failure to warn of danger, even though warnings,

---

[44] *Graham Barclay Oysters Pty Ld v Ryan; Ryan v Great Lakes Council; State of New South Wales v Ryan* [2002] HCA 54. The action succeeded at first instance and received some support on appeal but was overturned in the High Court.

[45] *Romeo v Conservation Commission of the Northern Territory* (1998) 151 ALR 263.

the High Court of Australia ultimately concluded, would probably have been futile. Of course, we can all admit that this was inevitably a hard case for the judges and not one that I personally would welcome having to decide. Like many of the cases referred to in these lectures, it opposes a 'vulnerable victim', unlikely to have protected herself against the risk of serious injury through insurance, against an apparently less vulnerable public authority, faced with the unpalatable prospect of expensively fencing—in the instant case— a substantial length of cliff face or, more generally, rendering risk-proof many million acres of recreational public land. The case contrasts strangely with the decision in *Jolley v Sutton LBC*,[46] where the English House of Lords, reversing the Court of Appeal, held a local authority liable for a rather unlikely accident caused to and by a youth playing with a derelict boat lying on council land. This too raises the nightmare prospect of rendering risk-proof all land in local authority possession to which the public has access. What is really on trial in these cases is the inadequacy of health care services in an age when technological advances can make life so much easier for the severely injured yet are too expensive for individuals to afford.[47]

As Stapleton compellingly argues, the success of tort law depends on its 'appearance of being fair, sensible and *focused*',[48] which I take to mean that it should sit comfortably within its conceptual framework. The developments she describes distort the corrective justice framework, diluting the essence of bilateral relationships by pushing liability back to distant actors and straining notions of causation and proximity past breaking-point. The danger is accentuated because, in the modern regulatory state, the state intervenes at some point in almost every human activity, however private it may seem; to put this differently, almost every human activity is contingently capable of regulation.

---

[46] *Jolley v Sutton LBC* [2000] 1 WLR 1082.

[47] Lunz, 'Liability of Statutory Authority for Omissions' (1998) 6 *Torts LJ* 107, 111, commenting on *Romeo, Northern Sandblasting Pty Ltd v Harris* (1997) 146 ALR 572 and other public authority cases.

[48] Stapleton, in Birks, above note 42, at 83 (emphasis mine).

'Damages', argues Ripstein, 'serve to place a problem where it properly lies, that is, with the responsible party';[49] the success of this strategy depends, however, on identifying some body we take to be responsible. To quote Atiyah, 'If the public thinks—as some people seem to think—that ultimately the government is responsible for everything that happens in society, then the government (and other public bodies) are liable to get sued, whatever they do or fail to do'. The resultant 'blame culture' is motored by a 'strong financial incentive to blame others for loss or death or wrongful injury'.[50] *Dorset Yacht* set the state squarely in the liability frame. In today's society, where state intervention has come to be accepted as broadly legitimate, with failure to intervene seen as culpable and potentially blameworthy, the effect is to open the 'deep coffers' of the state to financial marauders, primarily private insurers, sharks lurking unseen in the deep waters beneath tort actions.[51]

### CULPABILITY AND DETERRENCE

Even if there is much general agreement amongst tort lawyers that compensation is the primary objective of tort law, this is not necessarily how public lawyers see the matter. For them, Dicey's doctrine of the rule of law is necessarily seminal and his principle of equality before the law, whether or not it seems acceptable, must be read as normative. Like Hogg, the leading modern authority on Crown liability, I believe that Dicey captures a fundamental attitude towards government and reflects 'a widely-held political ideal'.[52]

Based as it is on a personal relationship between individual public servants and individual members of the public, the personal liability doctrine neatly fits the paradigm of

---

[49] A. Ripstein, 'Some Recent Obituaries of Tort Law' (1998) 48 *UTLJ* 561, 573.

[50] P. S. Atiyah, *The Damages Lottery* (Oxford: Hart Publishing, 1997) at 139.

[51] T. Weir, 'Governmental Liability' [1989] *PL* 40.

[52] P. Hogg, *Liability of the Crown* (2nd edn, Toronto: Carswell, 1989) at 1–2.

corrective justice. To the modern tort lawyer, the emphasis on *personal* liability is, however, distinctly old-fashioned. Already, writing between the two world wars, Jennings was critical of Dicey for glossing over the growing volume of statutory powers vested in public officials.[53] Today the process has gone much further; it is no longer public *servants* but public *services* and public *authorities* that we want to hold accountable and whose funds we want to access. I cannot too often reiterate the extent to which the functions of the state have changed. The state has welfare functions. It is interventionist. There has been an enormous growth in supervisory and regulatory powers. This steady expansion of state power has come together with the trend in modern tort law that I have been describing to replace *personal* liability by an *impersonal* set of non-delegable obligations vested in systems, corporations, and institutions. In the context of deterrence, Dicey's ideas are questionable.

Dicey, who wrote before the modern systematization of judicial review, viewed the tort action as the *primary* means of calling officials to account.[54] Although he did not explicitly say so, he clearly assumed that the threat of personal responsibility to the courts deterred public officers from abuse of power. Like our modern Nolan standards,[55] Dicey's theory of personal liability makes an important normative statement about the conduct expected of public servants and officials. It is worth recalling too that Dicey wrote before *Donoghue v Stevenson* had been decided. For Dicey, the paradigm tort was trespass,[56] with its emphasis

[53] I. W. Jennings, *The Law and the Constitution* (5th edn, London: University of London Press, 1959) at 54–6. See similarly, E. C. S. Wade, 'Introduction' in A. V. Dicey, *Introduction to the Study of the Law of the Constitution* (10th edn, London: Macmillan, 1959) at lxxvi–lxxxvi.

[54] As in the classic case of *Cooper v Wandsworth Board of Works* (1863) 14 CB(NS) 180.

[55] See *First Report of the Nolan Committee on Standards in Public Life*, Cm 2850 (1995).

[56] *Entick v Carrington* (1765) 2 Wils. KB 275; *Leach v Money* (1765) 19 St. Tr. 1001; *Wilkes v Wood* (1763) 2 Wils. KB 203 (the 'General Warrant Cases'). In addition, Dicey makes reference to *Mostyn v Fabrigas* (1774) 1 Cowp. 161; *Musgrave v Pulido* (1879) 5 App. Cas. 102; *Governor Wall's Case* (1802) 28 St. Tr. 51; and *Philips v Eyre* (1867) LR 4 QB 225, rather special tort actions.

on deliberate wrongdoing and defence of 'lawful authority'. He wrote in the consciousness of a long tradition of exemplary damages in cases of oppressive, arbitrary, and unconstitutional action by government servants—a practice that still forms part of our public law tradition and has to a certain extent been accepted by the Law Commission.[57] But although Dicey's is undoubtedly a deterrent theory of liability, it is one in which the deterrence is symbolic.

A more up-to-date theory of deterrence is that of Schuck,[58] who believes the award of damages against public officials creates 'perverse incentives'. Agencies, rather than individual actors, are best equipped to deter and should be held responsible.[59] In thinking about Schuck's theory, it must always be remembered that he writes within the American tradition of considerable state immunity at federal level.[60] Nevertheless, his analysis fits well with the general direction of modern tort law, characterized by the emphasis on *systemic* breakdown as a ground for negligence liability. Schuck's is really a theory of public service liability, based on the reasoning of economic rationalism.[61] He identifies six objectives for

---

[57] The position was expressly reserved by Lord Devlin in *Rookes v Barnard* [1964] AC 1129, restricted by the Court of Appeal in *Thompson v Commissioner of Metropolitan Police* [1998] QB 498, put out to consultation by the Law Commission, in its consultation paper on 'Aggravated, Exemplary and Restitutionary Damages', Law Com No 132 (1993) at paras 5.4–5.26 and 6.6–6.8. For the final recommendations, see 'Aggravated, Exemplary and Restitutionary Damages', Law Com No 247 (1997). The Law Commission wants to see punitive damages tightly regulated and in future largely confined to cases of deliberate and outrageous wrongdoing.

[58] P. Schuck, *Suing Government: Citizen Remedies for Official Wrongs* (New Haven, Conn.: Yale University Press, 1983) at 16–25.

[59] At 106–201.

[60] In ch 3, Schuck provides a valuable outline of the history and state of the contemporary law in the United States. The governing legislation is the Federal Tort Claims Act 1946. The extensive immunity has encouraged development of the notion of 'constitutional torts': see *Bivens v Six Unknown Named Agents of the Federal Bureau of Narcotics* 403 US 388 (1971).

[61] Coincidentally, Schuck's analysis resembles the French system of administrative liability, based on the impersonal notion of *faute de service*, on which see further D. Fairgrieve, *State Liability in Tort* (Oxford: Oxford University Press, 2003) 17–18, 21–3.

public law: (1) deterrence of wrongdoing, (2) promotion of vigorous decision-making, (3) compensation of victims, (4) exemplification of moral norms, (5) achievement of institutional competence and legitimacy, and (6) systemic efficiency through the integration of primary goals. These— and some escape the corrective justice paradigm—will, Schuck believes, be reinforced by extending liability.

Three main arguments can be deployed against Schuck. Somewhat ironically, the first is the answer of economic rationalists, who dismiss deterrence in the case of public services, on the ground that the state is a 'defendant that is not subject to exogenous economic constraints'. Findings of liability thus do little more than 'add to the public tax burden'.[62] This, as we shall see in a later section of this lecture, is a wholly unrealistic picture, that fails entirely to take into account the way modern systems of public financial accountability actually operate. Taxation is not, as is suggested, simply increased to provide for liability judgments. The majority of public authorities, in particular hospitals and local authorities, where perhaps a majority of the claims will be felt, have to insure against liability and to find the premiums out of carefully calculated and already restricted budgets. Treasurers and public auditors provide 'exogenous financial constraints' and insurers will be as interested in the liability records of public authorities as will the boards of directors of private schools and hospitals.

The second is that of functionalists, who raise the objection that evidence of tort law's deterrent properties is unconvincing. A major empirical study, which set out to test the efficacy of the tort system in five separate activity areas, produced mixed signals.[63] All that can be said is that the deterrent properties of tort law seem strongest for traffic,

---

[62] Feldthusen, above note 40, at 16. D. Cohen, 'Regulating Regulators: the Legal Environment of the State' (1990) 40 *UTLR* 213 makes the additional point that government can re-allocate the losses to victims, as was done in *Burmah Oil v Lord Advocate* [1965] AC 75.

[63] D. Dewes, D. Duff, and M. Trebilcock, *Exploring the Domain of Accident Law, Taking the Facts Seriously* (New York: Oxford University Press, 1996). The areas of study were: traffic accidents, medical negligence, products liability, environment, and workplace accidents.

and weakest for environmentally related, accidents and also that the tort system fails badly as a compensation mechanism, performing only reasonably well for traffic accidents, less well in environmental cases, and badly in cases of medical malpractice. In general, the study reinforces the suspicion that tort law is ineffective as a deterrent. As Braithwaite, writing of regulation, observes, 'deterring abuse of power, be it private or public, is not something we are good at. Problems of police corruption, dumping hazardous wastes and corporate fraud seem to bounce back after each wave of scandal and reform'.[64] Experience with the police, where liability is well established, buttressed by jury trial and by the long tradition of awarding exemplary damages, certainly suggests that tort law is inadequate as a regulator. One reason is the practice of out-of-court settlements, which screen wrongdoers from accountability. Police forces in particular seem able to fund settlements without too many questions being asked, though the payouts add up to substantial sums.

Against Schuck, it has also been strongly argued that government enterprises are less likely than private institutions to 'respond appropriately' to threats of liability, the likely response being only a 'greater dose of bureaucratic inertia'.[65] What tort law does is to create 'decision traps' that, by submitting decision-makers to competing pressures, produce a serious freezing effect on administrative action. The insertion of a liability decision into the decision-making process will have the effect of rendering policy- and decision-making more difficult, less effective, and certainly less 'rational', as irrelevant factors—fear of publicity or notably the threat of litigation—are taken into account and may override more relevant factors. This outcome is acceptable only if one believes—as I do not—in the efficiency of tort law as a regulator. Take the case of the police service,

---

[64] J. Braithwaite, 'On Speaking Softly and Carrying Big Sticks: Neglected Dimensions of a Republican Separation of Powers' (1997) 47 *UTLJ* 305, 360.

[65] Cass, 'Damages Suits Against Public Officers' 129 *University of Pennsylvania L Rev.* 1110 (1981).

aware perhaps of the presence in their area of someone on the sexual offenders register,[66] or the possible presence of a serial rapist;[67] whether or not to issue a public warning is a decision fraught with difficulty. Competing human rights have to be taken into consideration and the risks of precipitate action weighed against the risks of doing nothing. This is sufficiently complex without the risk of litigation as a complicating factor. Moreover, the award of damages in such cases is often frankly punitive and no account is taken of the possible 'chilling effects' on decision-taking.[68] This is part of a wider argument about 'polycentric decisions', seen as unsuitable for adjudication because of their potential 'spin off' effect.[69]

The inherent difficulty of the decisions involved and sensitivity to the 'decision trap' phenomenon led the judiciary to accept that, in the public interest, it would not be 'fair, just and reasonable' to impose liability in negligence on police officers engaged in the investigation of crime[70] or social workers exercising statutory powers and duties under the Children Acts. This was spelled out most clearly in *X (Minors) v Bedfordshire*,[71] a difficult case, where the House of Lords unfortunately had before them two sets of joined cases, very different in character. The first set, where the House of Lords thought liability possible, was brought to test the liability of local education authorities for systemic failures to diagnose and deal with the special educational

---

[66] *R v Chief Constable of North Wales ex p AB* (1998) 3 WLR 57.

[67] *Doe v Metropolitan Toronto Board of Commissioners of Police* (1989) 58DLR (4th) 396 affirmed (1990) 74 OR (2d) 225. The case is discussed further below.

[68] Compare the conflicting views of Childs and Ceyssens, '*Doe v Metropolitan Toronto Board of Commissioners of Police* and the Status of Public Oversight of the Police in Canada' (1998) 36 *Alberta L Rev.* 1000 and L. Hoyano, 'Policing Flawed Police Investigations: Unravelling the Blanket' (1999) 62 *MLR* 912, noting *Osman*, below at note 73.

[69] L. Fuller, 'The Forms and Limits of Adjudication' 92 *Harv. L Rev.* 353 (1978). See also J. Allison, 'The Procedural Reason for Judicial Restraint' [1994] *PL* 452 and 'Fuller's Analysis of Polycentric Disputes and the Limits of Adjudication' (1994) 53 *Cambridge LJ* 367.

[70] *Hill v Chief Constable of Yorkshire* [1988] 2 All ER 238.

[71] *X (Minors) v Bedfordshire Country Council, M v Newham London Borough Council* [1995] 2 AC 633 .

needs. The second set, which failed the 'fair, just, and reasonable' test of negligence, dealt with the potential liability of social workers exercising statutory powers designed for the protection of children under a series of Children Acts.

The linking factor in these otherwise disparate cases is that they all contain complex issues of polycentricity, centring on resources and 'decision traps'. Resources for education are finite. Resources for special educational needs are severely limited and have to be rationed; many pupils suffer from the lack of facilities that are simply not available. Moreover, a child who has not been diagnosed as dyslexic loses an unquantifiable set of chances: she might or might not have received appropriate remedial help from which she might or might not have benefited. Found liable, the education authority will have to consider whether to pay more on insurance; dismiss a teacher to take on another educational psychologist; or even to close down the facility. Courts have traditionally sought to avoid such questions on the ground that they lack experience, expertise, and, generally speaking, information. Yet many modern cases raise the spectre of open-ended financial commitment, either in the shape of compensation to a class of persons similarly affected or to revitalize public services found to have failed.

Studies of the effect of tort law on public decision-making are uncommon, inconclusive, and sometimes unreliable and such information as we do possess is fragmentary. Even if not directly transferable, one study of the United States Environmental Protection Agency is suggestive. The researcher found that court decisions now shape the policy agenda of the Agency, with results that are far from positive. 'In a climate of limited resources, coupled with unrealistic and numerous statutory mandates,' she asserts, 'the EPA has been forced to make decisions amongst competing priorities. With few exceptions, court orders have become the "winners" in this competition.'[72] If judicial

---

[72] R. O'Leary, *Environmental Change: Federal Courts and the EPA* (Philadelphia, Penn.: Temple Press, 1993), cited in D. Rosenbloom and R. O'Leary, *Public Administration and Law* (2nd edn, New York: Marcel Dekker, 1996) at 315.

decision-making were scientific and certain, this might be acceptable. But modern tort law is a process of water dripping on sandstone. After the *Osman* case,[73] for example, where the ECtHR insisted that litigants must receive some consideration on the merits of the case, a minor flood of cases resulted,[74] where the possibility of damages in actions by foster-parents, children, parents, and employees of social service departments was endlessly tested and re-tested. In the latest of these cases to reach the Court of Appeal, *JD and others v East Berkshire*,[75] the Court, after trawling one more time through the case law, ruled that *X v Bedfordshire* could not survive the Human Rights Act; it will thus no longer be legitimate to rule that, as a matter of law, no duty is owed to a child the subject of a suspected child abuse because *each case will fall to be decided on its individual facts*. It follows that no decision can be seen as really final; there is always a different plaintiff, a different fact situation, and a different defendant from among the many services and officials—social workers, schools, police, doctors, and clinics—involved. The East Berkshire case concerned a cluster of child abuse cases, some brought by parents accused of child abuse, others by children taken into care. The Court drew a bright-line between children, to whom a duty was owed, and parents, who were not sufficiently proximate for a duty to exist. In the light of recent revelations concerning the fallibility of scientific evidence in child abuse cases,[76]

---

[73] *Osman v United Kingdom* (1998) 29 EHRR 245.

[74] E.g., *W v Essex CC* [1998] 3 WLR 534; *Barrett v Enfield LBC* [1999] 3 WLR 79. On these and other cases, see: P. Craig and D. Fairgrieve, 'Barrett, Negligence and Discretionary Powers' [1999] *PL* 626; W. Murphy, 'Children in Need: the Limits of Local Authority Accountability' (2003) 23 *Legal Studies* 103. See also *Phelps v Hillingdon London Borough Council* [2000] 3 WLR 776 noted in D. Fairgrieve and M. Andenas, 'Tort Liability for Educational Malpractice: the *Phelps* Case (1999) 10 *KCLJ* 210.

[75] *JD and others v East Berkshire Community Health Trust and others* [2003] EWCA Civ 1151 at para 84.

[76] Doubts cast on the very existence of 'Munchausen's syndrome by proxy', resulted in the acquittal by the Court of Appeal of several mothers wrongfully convicted. This reopened the validity of thousands of care orders and adoptions. But see *Re U (A Child); Re B (A Child) (Serious Injury. Standard of Proof)* [2004] EWCA Civ 567.

who can believe this bright-line will be final? It is simply waiting to be distinguished on its facts. New cases are doubtless already in the pipeline waiting to overtake it, and the question is only, how long will it endure?

This process of incremental extension by what Atiyah terms 'selective comparison' with cases that have suc-ceeded or nearly succeeded[77] leaves decision-makers in a hopeless quandary. They are left to guess at possible judi-cial reaction to unpredictable happenings that have not yet taken place in the sure and certain knowledge that judges always have the benefit of hindsight and the last word. The position is exacerbated by the fluid and unpredictable nature of the 'fair, just, and reasonable' test, a euphemistic way of describing virtually unstructured judicial discretion. Sometimes judges apply the 'vulnerable victim' test from tort law and favour a near universal obligation to protect all children from every risk of harm. Sometimes they remem-ber that a common law duty of care would 'cut across the entire statutory system set up for the protection of children at risk', encouraging defensive decision-making, breeding ill-will in already difficult relationships, diverting money and resources 'away from the performance of the social service for which they were provided'.[78] We might add that an action for damages is a very poor weapon for inves-tigating whether public bodies have behaved well or badly. For those responsible for carrying on difficult and perenni-ally underfunded public services under the scrutiny of auditors and ombudsmen, such judicial zig-zagging has severe implications.

### TAKING DICEY SERIOUSLY

The third argument against Schuck's deterrent theory is a wider argument against all rules and liability principles that treat the state as special. Cohen, for example, observ-

---

[77] Atiyah, *The Damages Lottery*, above note 50.
[78] *S v Gloucestershire County Council* [2001] 1 Fam 313, 329.

ing the 'enormous growth of the supervisory and wealth-redistributing function of the modern state', sees 'twentieth-century governments, regardless of political colour, [as] consequently engaged in a range of interventionist activities *which have no private analogues'*.[79] From this he deduces that to define liability in terms of interindividual relationships is 'to ignore the state'. But state and government, we have learned, are not static concepts[80] nor is the public/private boundary fixed immutably. Virtually every service designated 'public' and every function indelibly associated with the state, with the possible exception of national security, has at one time or another been privately performed. Trenchantly making this point, Freeman mentions in the United States fire protection, welfare provision, education, and policing, all currently in this country the subject of significant tort litigation; roads, bridges, railways, and sewers were built mainly by private contractors, hoping to profit from their enterprises.[81]

The dynamics of the current situation are nicely exemplified in the recent case of *Marcic v Thames Water*.[82] The Marcic garden was one of a number regularly washed by sewage, freely provided by Thames Water, a privatized commercial company, providing a public service. Fed up with inaction, Marcic, who had spent a considerable sum on amelioration, requested damages for loss of amenity and for consequential diminution in the value of his property. Invoking a number of precedents where, in similar circumstances, water authorities had been exempted from strict

[79] D. Cohen, 'Tort Law and the Crown: Administrative Compensation and the Modern State' in K. Cooper-Stephenson and E. Gibson (eds), *Tort Theory* (York: Captus University Publications, 1993) at 366 (emphasis mine).

[80] M. Taggart, 'The Nature and Functions of the State' in P. Cane and M. Tushnet (eds), *The Oxford Handbook of Legal Studies* (Oxford: Oxford University Press, 2003).

[81] J. Freeman, 'The Private Role in Public Governance' 75 *NY Univ. L Rev.* 543, 552–3 (2000).

[82] *Marcic v Thames Water Utilities Ltd* [2002] QB 929 (CA); [2003] 3 WLR 1603 (HL). For the damages assessment, see *Marcic v Thames Water (No 2)* [2002] QB 1003 (Judge Haverey QC).

liability in nuisance,[83] Thames Water refused either to compensate the plaintiff or to terminate the nuisance. The Court of Appeal was happy to bring the immunity to an end, ruling that the flooding amounted to a nuisance, which Thames Water had adopted and for which it was liable. The Court brushed aside objections as to cost, prioritization, and effective resource allocation, suggesting that the 'fair, just, and reasonable' test could somehow slice through any problems. It was, they thought, *at least arguable* that 'those who make use of the sewerage system should be charged sufficient to cover the cost of paying compensation to the minority who suffer damage as a consequence of the operation of the system'.[84]

For proponents of the public/private boundary, the change could be seen as fully justifiable. The exception, based on the idea of 'general benefit of the community', had been established at a time when sewerage and water supply were the responsibility of public water authorities, in practice usually the local authority. It had lasted throughout a period of public ownership, when liability could accurately be said to consume public funds. Since 1991, however, the water industry has been privatized, at which point the rule fell to be reconsidered. This line of reasoning is reflected in the speech of Lord Nicholls, who thought the imposition of liability in nuisance to be wholly incompatible with the modern statutory scheme. Antiquated rules, designed to regulate relations between neighbouring landowners, were not applicable to a methodical plan for the supply of water to the community as a whole and for a country-wide system for sewage disposal. The same line was taken by Lord Hoffmann, though drawn once again

---

[83] See *Glossop v Heston and Isleworth Local Board* (1879) 12 Ch. D 102; *Dixon v Metropolitan Board of Works* (1881) 7 QBD 418; *Strettons Derby Brewers v Derby Corporation* (1894) 1 Ch. 431; *Robinson v Workington Corporation* (1897) 1 QB 619; *Smeaton v Ilford Corporation* [1954] Ch. 450. As these cases suggest, the water authority was in practice during the late nineteenth century normally the local authority. See generally M. Brazier (ed), *Clerk and Lindsell on Torts* (17th edn, London: Sweet and Maxwell, 1995) ch 18.

[84] [2002] QB at para 114.

to the simplistic public/private bright-line which so often underlies his reasoning. Capital expenditure by a statutory public utility, he argued, involves very different considerations from those raised by a bipolar relationship between two adjacent landowners. Where the latter are in issue, it was the court's duty, whatever the difficulties, to perform its usual function of deciding what is reasonable between the two parties:[85]

But the exercise becomes very different when one is dealing with capital expenditure of a statutory undertaking providing public utilities on a large scale.... If one customer is given a certain level of services, everyone in the same circumstances should receive the same level of services. So the effect of a decision about what it would be reasonable to expect a sewerage undertaker to do for the plaintiff is extrapolated across the country.

Let us explore this reasoning a little further. It must be admitted that, even if the privatized water authorities are primarily profit-making corporations, there are clear limits to their horizons. Buckley, who leans towards liability, admits in a comment that 'the resources even of such organisations are not unlimited; and the continuing statutory framework within which they operate, under the supervision of the Office of Water Services, serves to highlight that their investment decisions will sometimes be as much economic and social as commercial'.[86] The supply of water is a form of collective consumption. Water authorities, along with most other public utility suppliers, carry out public service functions and have to balance aggregative and distributive or individual interests in the delivery of services. Less tangible factors, such as environmental protection, must also be taken into account. Typically, these private, profit-making agencies operate with a blend of public and private funding. They are supervised and monitored by regulatory agencies and are, in the case of the water industry, regulated as to charges, which require the approval of the regulator. Investment calculations have to

[85] At para 63.
[86] R. A. Buckley, 'Nuisance and the Public Interest' (2002) 118 LQR 508, 510.

unite a concern for shareholders' dividends with community interest.

With some force, Buckley argues that profit-making organizations ought to be submitted 'to the full rigour of
private law disciplines'.[87] This conclusion seems to be
premised on two underlying assumptions: first, that public
bodies are not or not *always* to be made liable to 'the full
rigours of private law', a clear defiance of the parity
principle; the second, that public bodies act always in the
public interest, while private corporations are activated
solely by profit motives, fallacious logic also latent in Lord
Hoffmann's reasoning. Highly relevant is the case law on
which Lord Hoffmann is commenting. In *Leakey v National
Trust*,[88] the Trust was found liable to prevent a natural land-
slip arising in a Saxon burial mound. Could it not be argued
that the Trust, as custodian of an object of great archaeological value, was acting in the public interest and that the
finding of liability was likely to have a most unfortunate
impact on its conservation activities and also those of lesser
landowners in a similar position? Many years earlier, the
House of Lords had imposed a rather different obligation
on the nationalized rail industry when considering the
duties of landowners towards trespassers on their land. In
that case, which observes the parity rule, the standard of
care expected is said to be variable according to the defendant's size and resources.[89]

The main thrust of Buckley's argument, however, concerns accountability. Defined as a public body, an agency is
legally accountable in two separate ways: through an application for judicial review and, in civil law, through a tort
action. In sharp contrast, the 'private' label may, if tort law
proves inapplicable, carry immunity. While water authorities remained in the public sector, their decisions could
be challenged by judicial review; transferred to the private
sector, judicial review proceedings might no longer be
available. In the instant case, Parliament has supplied the

[87] R. A. Buckley, 'Nuisance and the Public Interest' (2002) 118 LQR
508, 510
[88] *Leakey v National Trust* [1980] 1 All ER 17.
[89] *Herrington v British Railways Board* [1972] AC 877.

answer: a statutory complaints procedure is available to householders in Mr Marcic's position and, in pursuing his claim in damages, Mr Marcic was seeking to sidestep the statutory enforcement code; the fact that he had declined to use the statutory procedures weighed heavily against him in the House of Lords.[90] In other cases, the absence of alternative remedies could leave an accountability gap. Agreed: but surely the failure lies on the judicial review side of the line? Many commentators have persuasively argued that the ambit of judicial review should be extended.[91]

'Contracting out' has multiplied, and privatization complicated, the multiple links between public and private sectors; commercial enterprises may be entrusted with paradigm public functions, as in the case of private prisons and detention centres. Should liability vary when Group 4 rather than the Home Office operates the prison or immigration services? Staff transfer regularly between the sectors and may practise simultaneously in both, as do general practitioners, specialists, and surgeons in the health sector, where agency nursing staff prop up the NHS. Vaccines and drugs supplied by private commercial companies are used in public programmes, regulated by the terms of contracts drawn up by the state for which they have tendered publicly; should liability vary, for example, according to whether defective blood used in blood transfusions was supplied through the National Health Service or a commercial enterprise?[92] Nor should one assume that commercial enterprises are necessarily entirely privately funded. The railways, for example, started life in the private sector; were nationalized and transferred to government; and then

---

[90] [2003] 3 WLR paras 21–22, 35, 43, 51–52, 79–82. S. 18 of the Water Act 1991 provides for complaints to be made to the regulator of the water industry, who may then take enforcement proceedings.

[91] Suggestions for a systematized realignment in a sense relevant to my argument are to be found in J. Black, 'Constitutionalising Self-regulation' (1996) 59 *MLR* 24.

[92] Consider *A and others v The National Blood Authority* [2001] 3 All ER 289 noted by G. Howells and M. Mildred, 'Infected Blood: Defect and Discoverability, A First Exposition of the EC Product Liability Directive' (2002) 65 *MLR* 95.

privatized. Today they are being quietly re-nationalized: Network Rail is to all intents and purposes a nationalized industry; up to 50 per cent of train operators receive substantial levels of state subsidy; and 25 per cent are run by an autonomous agency, the Strategic Rail Authority. On the other side of the line, Eurostar is a private, commercial company, heavily in debt and regularly bailed out by vast inputs of public money. This is not a context in which 'special' rules of liability applicable to the state are likely to flourish.

Equally, rule-making, a classical governmental function, may be exercised by private bodies. This was remarked when the British Boxing Board of Control was held liable for negligence in the exercise of its rule-making functions, for failure to set in place and maintain adequate safety regulations.[93] Should liability for standard-setting or rule-making differ *merely because* the regulator is the Health and Safety Executive, a statutory agency exercising statutory functions?

More pertinent is the banking sector, where the supervisory responsibility of the autonomous Bank of England over the activities of private banks was recently tested in the *Three Rivers* case, under the rubric of misfeasance in public office.[94] These functions did not differ greatly from those exercised (or not exercised) by the Department of Trade and Industry, examined some years earlier in the Barlow Clowes affair, which led to a major ombudsman inquiry and state compensation scheme after a private 'bond

---

[93] *Watson v British Boxing Board of Control* [2001] 2 WLR 1256, noted by J. George, 'Watson v British Boxing Board of Control: Negligent Rule-making in the Court of Appeal' (2002) 65 *MLR* 106. *Marc Rich & Co v Bishop Rock Marine Co Ltd* [1996] AC 211 gives a more satisfactory answer.

[94] *Three Rivers District Council v Governor and Company of the Bank of England* [1996] 3 All ER 558; [2000] 2 WLR 1220. See M. Andenas and D. Fairgrieve, 'Misfeasance in Public Office, Governmental Liability, and European Influences' (2002) 51 *ICLQ* 757. The case is continuing and the hearing is likely to go on for a further year, costing many millions. For similar problems in France, see Annex below.

washing' dealer failed.[95] To introduce the complication of separate rules of liability based purely on the public character of regulatory functions is wilfully to throw away the advantages of our flexible, unitary jurisdiction.

The question whether public authorities are to be held accountable for the exercise of statutory powers and duties is logically separate, as many great judges have insisted,[96] from the question of duty of care. Yet the two questions have become hopelessly entangled. Remarking on the misleading tendency to talk of a 'common law duty *superimposed upon* statutory powers', Gaudron J pointed out—in the Australian High Court[97]—that statute always operates 'in the milieu of the common law' so that the common law applies to that body unless excluded. One might deduce that the question of exclusion ought to be left expressly to the legislator. Unfortunately, however, generations of judges have taken a wrong fork, reasoning instead that '[e]ven if the legislation does not do so in terms, the nature or purpose of the powers and functions conferred, or of some of them, may be such as to give rise to an *inference* that it was intended that the common law should be excluded either in whole or part'.[98] The concepts to which judges have turned in drawing these inferences, for the most part involving distinctions between discretionary powers and mandatory duties, public and private law, and policy and operational decisions, have proved profoundly disappointing.

---

[95] See Report by the Parliamentary Commissioner for Administration, 'The Barlow Clowes Affair', HC 76 (1989/90). See too Report by the Parliamentary Commissioner for Administration, 'The Prudential Regulation of Equitable Life', HC 809 (2002/3) on the responsibilities of the Financial Services Authority as 'prudential regulator' in respect of insurers after the failure of Equitable Life.

[96] Notably Lord Atkin dissenting in *East Suffolk Catchment Board v Kent* [1941] AC 74; Lord Reid in *Home Office v Dorset Yacht* [1970] AC 1004; and Lord Salmon in *Anns v Merton LBC* [1978] AC 728.

[97] *Crimmins v Stevedoring Committee* (1999) 200 CLR 1, noted by Bowman and S. Bailey 'Public Authority Negligence on the Waterfront' (2001) 9 *Tort Law Rev.* 7.

[98] (1999) 200 CLR 1 at para 27.

Thus, in an attempt to protect the discretionary or 'policy' element in public decision-making, courts in some cases have introduced the concept of 'operational negligence', seen as more appropriate than policy as an area for liability. Since decisions are more often arrived at than taken, the search for the moment of decision has proved entirely futile. As Prosser has observed,[99] there is 'no moment of decision to which one can point and say, "Aha, there policy was made!" or "There policy was implemented"'. For Cohen all bureaucratic decision-making is 'both policy and operational in nature. That is, any particular instance of public action can be seen as implementing a superior decision—and this could even be said of legislative action intended to make operational a prior executively defined public policy choice'.[100] But what is specifically public about these descriptions of bureaucratic decision-making? They are applicable across the board, to public and private bureaucracies alike. In multinational corporations, for example, decisions may be formally 'taken' by a board of directors and 'implemented' by the managing director and the vast staff at his disposal, but equally it can be said that the board merely 'implements' policies put to it by the managing director.

Categories, Feldthusen reminds us, are always arbitrary and their value is 'less in their logic than their utility'.[101] There is no magic in the public/private distinction, and the use made of it in tort law is unconvincing.[102] That the state, government, or Crown 'cannot be equated with an individual [because] the Crown represents the State'[103] is a truism.

---

[99] T. Prosser, 'Social Limits to Privatizing' 21 *Brook J of International Law* 213 (1995).

[100] D. Cohen, 'Tort Law and the Crown: Administrative Compensation and the Modern State' in K. Cooper-Stephenson and E. Gibson (eds), *Tort Theory* (York: Captus University Publications, 1993) at 363.

[101] B. Feldthusen, 'The Recovery of Pure Economic Loss in Canada: Proximity, Justice, Rationality and Chaos' (1996) 24 *Manitoba LJ* 1, 2.

[102] C. Harlow, '"Public" and "Private" Law: Definition Without Distinction' (1980) 43 *MLR* 241.

[103] *Rudolph Wolff & Co. Ltd. and Noranda Inc. v The Crown* [1990] 1 SCR 695; 69 DLR (4th) 392.

The message conveyed is that the state is somehow 'special' but there is no deeper explanation of *why* this should be so. Why should collective political responsibility somehow preclude legal liability to individuals? That is simply to breathe life into the antiquated folklore of a Crown that 'can do no wrong'. It does not follow logically from the fact that the state represents the interests of all members of society—which, incidentally, it patently does not—that the parity rule to which we pay lip service should not apply. Behind every tort action lie the same policy questions: Why is it 'fair, just and reasonable' in this situation to impose liability? What elements of the case point to liability or non-liability and how should they be balanced? What makes this case special enough to justify exemption? These questions need to be answered frankly and directly. The public/private distinction is a 'boiler plate answer', a formalist brush-off.

To elucidate the point I have been making, I should like to conclude this lecture by considering one of the big cases in which the public/private distinction played a part. In *Stovin v Wise*,[104] a traffic accident occurred when the first defendant turned negligently out of a blind junction, previously identified by the highway authority as an accident black spot. The council as highway authority had contacted British Rail, the landowner, for permission to carry out modifications but subsequently failed to notice that no reply had been received and to follow the matter up. Although this error was clearly operational, the courts were uncomfortable because the non-exercise of statutory powers was involved. Had a lawful, resource or risk-based decision *not* to take action been taken, the accident might still have occurred. The case was thus said to lie 'at the interface of public and private law'. For Lord Nicholls, this was not a problem; the council had 'failed to fulfil its public law obligations just as much as if it were in breach of a statutory

---

[104] *Stovin v Wise (Norfolk CC, third party)* [1996] 3 WLR 388, noted by J. Convery, 'Public or Private? Duty of Care in a Statutory Framework: *Stovin v Wise* in the House of Lords' (1997) 60 *MLR* 559.

duty'. He saw the public law elements and 'typical statutory framework' as *easing* the step to a common law duty to
act, by helping to create a 'proximity which would not
otherwise exist'.[105] Lord Hoffmann, speaking for the majority, made the entirely opposite deduction that 'arguments
peculiar to public bodies' might *negative* the existence of a
duty of care. He simply discarded the inconvenient policy/
operational distinction as 'an inadequate tool', arguing that,
even if a clearly operational error were found, it did not
necessarily follow that liability should be imposed.[106]

This case does not stretch the corrective justice framework as far as the regulatory and supervisory cases men-
tioned earlier. It is, all the same, a case to which insurance
was crucial; it may, indeed, have been brought, as many
similar cases are, solely to decide whose insurers were
going to foot the bill. Lord Nicholls tacitly admits this,
asking whether anything of social utility is to be gained by
shifting the financial loss from road users to a highway
authority?[107] Compulsory third party traffic insurance is a
fact of common knowledge and points to the conclusion
that losses caused by road accidents ought, so far as possible, to fall on the insurer which has taken premiums to
cover the risk of accident; only in very exceptional cases
should it be transferred to the highway authority, however
lax and careless that authority has been. Such a solution
would, to economic rationalists, be 'fair, just, and reasonable' though this is not terminology they are likely to use.
Why should the taxpayer foot the insurer's bill? Remedial
action inside the administrative system is best suited to
deter operational error. We should not without good reason
ask the state to guarantee insurers, even if we know that
awards of damages made against private commercial enterprises may in practice become a state responsibility when
insurers (or employers) go bankrupt, just as other losses
caused by the failure of insurers or banks may be accepted
by the state. But wait a minute! Is not Lord Nicholls' entirely

---

[105] [1996] 3 WLR at 392, 398.        [106] Ibid., at 404.
[107] Ibid., at 403.

contrary conclusion that the community is 'entitled to expect better from a public authority'[108] equally 'fair, just, and reasonable'? It simply prioritizes the deterrent goals of tort law, a subject on which I have said enough.

## CONCLUSION

In this lecture, I have essentially presented two parallel sets of arguments. The first set concerns the nature of the state and society. I have noted the emergence of a society imbued with the values of consumerism and trained in the individualist ideology of human rights, with consequential implications for tort law. I have described the state as an evolutionary phase between the residual state, for which Dicey's doctrine of equality through personal liability was adequate, through the socialist welfare state of public services where accident compensation would have been logical, to the modern capitalist, interventionist, regulatory state. In the process, I have argued forcefully against the complication of a public/private liability distinction and for the parity principle as normative.

The second set of arguments concerns the tort law that has developed in these contexts. I have reflected on the corrective justice paradigm of tort law, from which I think we are unwise to stray too far. I have fixed on the *Dorset Yacht* case as the starter motor of state liability and questioned the way in which it has evolved to place the state in the position of guarantor. All that I am saying for the present about cases involving public authorities is that the problems they pose are undoubtedly difficult. They are, however, not exceptional in character. They are, to put this differently, no more problematic than tort law itself.

---

[108] Ibid., at 396.

# 2

# Tort Law Abounding

## THE CASCADE EFFECT OF GLOBALIZATION

So far, I have been talking about the state playing on its home ground, leaving international legal institutions and regimes on the sidelines. In the national context, I described our state primarily as a regulatory state, though with remaining welfare functions. I described the main trend of tort law as expansive. In this second lecture, I want to consider the effects of globalization on national systems of tort law. I shall argue that globalization, with its effect of 'speeding up and deepening [the] impact of transcontinental flows and patterns of social interaction',[1] is producing a 'cascade effect', whereby developments in one legal system are coming routinely to influence and trigger change in others.

States are not, of course, the only or even the most important players on the transnational circuit; there are many powerful global players anxious to join the game. Some, like the World Trade Organization, European Union and its influential Court of Justice, and the Strasbourg Court of Human Rights, have set themselves up as referees, using law to augment their standing and extend their field of play. The increased sophistication and reach of international law is bringing new bids for referee status, while the rapid diffusion of a human rights culture strongly rooted in law has in some cases impinged quite heavily on national systems of tort law, sometimes at the behest of national judges.[2] This spread of the ambit and influence

---

[1] D. Held and A. McGrew, *Globalization/Anti-Globalization* (Cambridge: Polity Press, 2002) at 1.

[2] A. Mason, 'Human Rights Law and the Law of Torts' in P. Cane and J. Stapleton (eds), *The Law of Obligations, Essays in Celebration of John Fleming* (Oxford: Clarendon, 1998). And see the essays in C. Scott (ed), *Torture as Torts* (Oxford: Hart Publishing, 2000).

of international and transnational jurisdictions is said by those who welcome globalization to be part of a very necessary reconfiguration of political power in the modern world. This, I shall argue, is to downplay and overlook the not entirely beneficial secondary effects of globalization.

I am not, of course, about to argue that there is anything unhealthy in a process of interchange and experimentation (as some comparativists prefer to call it, cross-fertilization).[3] I recognize that there is nothing new in a trade in legal ideas. Unlike the more extreme prophets of globalization, however, I have reservations about the practice and extent of legal transplant. Legal concepts and principles are being treated as a form of technology, transferable, like mobile telephones, from one culture to another. Unlike cell phones, however, legal orders are embedded in constitutional and political systems and fill a particular slot within that system. They possess their own particular structure and ethos and may be affected by translation in unexpected and unwanted ways.[4] Coherence, consistency, and stability are essential features of any stable legal system, as I suggested when considering the corrective justice model of tort law. Discrimination is needed in the game of legal transplant if the coherence of the legal system is not to be damaged; metaphorically speaking, legal transplants are capable of behaving like the rampant cane toad when thoughtlessly introduced into Australia, or running wild, like Japanese knotweed in the English countryside.

---

[3] E.g., J. Bell, 'Mechanisms for Cross-fertilisation of Administrative Law in Europe' in J. Beatson and T. Tridimas (eds), *New Directions in European Public Law* (Oxford: Hart Publishing, 1998).

[4] For an extension of this argument, see C. Harlow, 'Voices of Difference in a Plural Community' in P. Beaumont, C. Lyons, and N. Walker (eds), *Convergence and Divergence in European Public Law* (Oxford: Hart Publishing, 2002). And see R. Cotterell, 'The Symbolism of Constitutions' in I. Loveland (ed), *A Special Relationship? American Influences on Public Law in the UK* (Oxford: Clarendon, 1995). For a more extreme version of the argument, maintaining the virtual impossibility of harmonizing common law and civilian legal systems, see A. Legrand, 'European Legal Systems Are Not Converging' (1996) 45 *ICLQ* 52, who uses the term *mentalité* to express the ethos or deep values of a legal system.

In my first lecture, I supported the argument that tort law's rapid expansion was distorting the theoretical framework of the corrective justice model. But tort law is as much a remedy or cause of action as a set of concepts. In this lecture, I shall abandon the conceptual ground to argue that globalization is creating pressure to expand the circumstances in which pecuniary compensation is recoverable from the state. Not every judicial toolkit contains the positive remedies of mandatory orders or damages, and this may be for good reason. There is not one rule of law but many: judicial orders do not all occupy the same space in the system of governance, nor do they necessarily need to operate identically.[5] Globalization is fostering a competitive attitude to legal remedies and tempting judges, especially when human rights are in issue, to move from negative to affirmative remedies. Negative remedies set limits, telling legislators when they are offside. Affirmative remedies are more intrusive, imposing penalties or, more intrusive still, ordering governments to intervene positively in society to secure affirmative rights. Affirmative rights, which relate closely to the concept of distributive justice,[6] are rights which impose affirmative duties on governments to intervene to redress deprivations in society. There is a close link here with the economic and social rights increasingly represented in modern human rights documents.[7] A feeling is growing up that affirmative rights require affirmative remedies and that every 'real' court should possess them. Courts are racing to complete their 'toolkit'. Against the trend, I shall argue in this lecture that this general ratcheting-up of remedies is as undesirable as the unconsidered expansion of tort law, and that it needs to be restrained.

---

[5] An argument advanced compellingly in a defence of French administrative law by Abraham, 'Les principes généraux de la protection juridictionnelle administrative en Europe: L'influence des jurisprudences européennes' (1997) 9 *European Review of Public Law* 577.

[6] Above, Introduction, text at note 5.

[7] H. Lessard, 'The Idea of "Private": A Discussion of State Action Doctrine and Separate Sphere Ideologies' (1986) 10 *Dalhousie LJ* 197.

The impact of globalization was first felt keenly in product liability cases, where the developing pattern of global trading ultimately made it possible for a single product, released on to a mass market by one or more manufacturers, to trigger claims around the world. Strict liability for products gained ground in the United States during the 1960s and early 1970s,[8] and soon percolated into other systems, leading to the introduction of statutory strict liability regimes.[9] Accident compensation also assumed a global aspect, with fear of liability from air crashes or nuclear accidents prompting global solutions, often through the medium of an international liability convention.[10] It may have been with the Bhopal chemical explosion disaster that tort law's international dimension began to float to the surface of the public consciousness, when the spectacle of American lawyers flying in to sign up clients and returning home to serve writs in US courts received wide publicity. The disaster brought into question the responsibility of the American Union Carbide Corporation for an explosion in the factory of its Indian subsidiary, involving complex issues of corporate and private international law.[11] The Indian state soon became involved: by the Bhopal Act, the

---

[8] W. Prosser, 'The Assault on the Citadel (Strict Liability to the Consumer)' 69 *Yale LJ* 1099 (1960) and 'The Fall of the Citadel (Strict Liability to the Consumer)' 50 *Minnesota L Rev.* 791 (1966). See also E. White, *Tort Law in America, An Intellectual History* (Oxford: Oxford University Press, 1980) at 168–73; G. Schwartz, 'The Beginning and the Possible End of the Rise of Modern American Tort Law' 26 *Georgia L Rev.* 601 (1992); S. Sugarman, 'A Century of Change in Personal Injuries Law' 88 *California L Rev.* 2403 (2000).

[9] For the UK, the Consumer Protection Act 1988; for the European Union, Council Directive 85/374/EEC of 25 July 1985 on the approximation of the laws, regulations and administrative provisions of the MSS concerning liability for defective products [1985] OJ L210/29.

[10] The Warsaw Convention provides an exclusive cause of action for claims against an air carrier in cases of accident causing personal injury. The Convention is incorporated into British law by the Carriage by Air Act 1961, to which it is annexed: see *In Re Deep Vein Thrombosis* [2003] 3 WLR 961.

[11] P. Muchlinski, 'The Bhopal Case: Controlling Ultrahazardous Industrial Activities Undertaken by Foreign Investors' (1987) 50 *MLR* 545, 550–2.

Indian government set up a statutory scheme to regulate compensation claims. The Act gave the Indian government the sole right of representation in all claims arising from the accident and set up an administrative compensation scheme, together with a fund designed to meet costs. Limits were placed on rights of private action in the interests of a collective solution, a course of action sparking a constitutional controversy, referred to the Supreme Court of India. (This was incidentally a forerunner of many similar disputes now, as we shall see, routinely handled by transnational courts as a parasitic effect of the developing litigation culture.) Dissatisfaction was widespread, leading to further legal battles. These are discussed in the next section.

Under global pressure, tort law seemed to be developing into an affair of mass torts, class actions, consolidation, and representative actions. 'Forum shopping' became the order of the day, with the aim of obtaining for litigants (and their lawyers) the benefit of regimes with the highest damages or lowest costs; where punitive damages are available; where the rules of liability are most favourable to the plaintiff; or where limitation periods are longest. Judges as well as litigants now need to be alert to the international context, and pressure for standardization is created as judges seek to deter—or sometimes to encourage—forum shopping. At first the procedural devices to which courts and plaintiffs' lawyers turned to accommodate the mass litigation phenomenon were welcomed, at least by lawyers. Thus the Agent Orange case, brought by veterans to seek compensation for damage caused by the use of defoliants in the Vietnam War, involved millions of claims and was hailed as a breakthrough in class litigation.[12] Latterly, however, difficulties inherent in the management of mass litigation have become visible and a jungle of expensive and sterile procedural litigation, dispiriting for claimants, has de-

---

[12] The class was certified in *In re 'Agent Orange' Product Liability Litigation* 100 FRD 718 (EDNY 1983) affirmed in 81 F 2d 145 (2d circuit 1987). And see P. Schuck, *Agent Orange on Trial: Mass Toxic Disasters in the Courts* (Boston, Mass.: Harvard University Press, 1986), 132.

veloped.[13] On this side of the Atlantic, we have seen the system falter before serious internal warfare between sections of the class, as appetite for litigation or objectives began to diverge under strain.[14]

Already in 1987, John Fleming, doyen of comparative tort law, was expressing doubts over the ability of the tort system, operating through the method of case-by-case adjudication and with principles still largely premised on the 'corrective justice' model, to meet the challenge of mass torts.[15] When he wrote, asbestosis and tobacco litigation was in its infancy; some years later, the plethora of cases under way in courtrooms round the world would highlight the inadequacies of the mass tort action. The effects of globalization on the American legal system were traumatic; one academic commentator depicted the system as both 'taunted' and 'tormented' by asbestos litigation.[16] By 'taunting', the author meant that an asbestos injury claim is essentially a relatively uncomplicated tort 'of the sort handled by the civil liability system for many centuries', typically a products liability or employer's liability claim for personal injuries, and as such an answer should have been forthcoming from the tort action. The 'torment' arose from the realization that the US legal system was impotent before the volume of cases in the asbestos litigation. Statistics show that 500,000 asbestos workers and families have sued for damages in the last forty years; insurers have paid more than $20 billion, the final estimate being around

---

[13] S. Issacharoff, 'Governance and Legitimacy in the Law of Class Actions' [1999] *Supreme Court Rev.* 337.

[14] See the account of the UK thalidomide case: *Sunday Times* Insight Team, *Suffer The Children: The Story of Thalidomide* (London: Futura, 1979). And see generally J. C. Coffee, 'Class Action Accountability: Reconciling Exit, Voice and Loyalty in Representative Litigation' 100 *Col. L Rev.* 370 (2000) and 'Class Wars: The Dilemma of the Mass Tort Class Action' 95 *Col. L Rev.* 1343.

[15] J. Fleming, *The American Tort Process* (Oxford: Clarendon, 1987) at 235. See also D. Rosenberg, 'The Causal Connection in Mass Exposure Cases: A Public Law Vision of the Tort System' 97 *Harv. L Rev.* 851 (1984).

[16] S. Issacharoff, ' "Shocked": Mass Torts and Aggregate Asbestos Litigation After Amchem and Ortiz' 80 *Texas L Rev.* 1925 (2002).

$200 billion before the crisis is predicted to end around the year 2030.[17] The classical corrective justice model of the tort action is individuated, geared to litigation by individually represented individuals, whose expectation is that each case will be considered on its individual merits. The asbestos actions destroyed the model, reducing it to myth.

Significantly for my argument, mass tort cases are now processed in much the same way as statutory and administrative compensation schemes. It has, for example, been shown that plaintiffs in successful asbestos class actions got less than 40 per cent of the damages they claimed; perhaps a lesser windfall than state accident compensation would provide. Moreover, the claims resulted in up to forty bankruptcy petitions from the class of defendant corporations, a further factor in the scale of compensation received by plaintiffs. Finally, an essentially administrative process for resolving claims had to be proposed, which introduced an 'injury grid' with an accompanying scale of compensation awards. Significantly, punitive damages as an element in settlement were barred. Limited opportunities for recourse to arbitration or the courts were offered. This scheme, which sounds much like an administrative compensation plan, was designed and engineered by courts and later approved by them.[18] As judges in the asbestos litigation freely admitted, the class action is often an inefficient surrogate for the state. State or inter-state action is normally necessary for final resolution. Even then a final solution may ultimately be eluded. Not all the relatives of victims killed in the PanAm Lockerbie air crash or by the collapse of the twin towers of the World Trade Centre agreed to accept

---

[17] D. Hensler, 'As Time Goes By: Asbestos Litigation After *Amchem* and *Ortiz*' 80 *Texas L Rev.* 1899 (2002); D. Rosenberg, 'Individual Justice and Collectivising Risk-Based Claims in Mass Exposure Cases' 71 *NYUL Rev.* 210 (1996); D. Hensler *et al., Asbestos in the Courts: The Challenge of Mass Toxic Torts* (Santa Monica, Cal.: Institute for Civil Justice, 1985).

[18] Hensler, above note 17, at 1899, 1907, 1915. The arrangements for settlement were established by *Georgine v Amchem Products Inc* 157 FRD 246 (ED Pa 1994). *Ahearn v Fibreboard Corporation* 162 FRD 505 (ED Tex 1995) barred punitive damages in settlements.

the generous compensation. 'It's not about money,' one of the parties is reported as saying. 'The decision is whether you want to go the long haul and get answers under oath from people why it happened.'[19]

## ACCOUNTABILITY THROUGH LIABILITY

It is all very well for systematizing academics to decide that tort law is the preserve of corrective justice, or for judges to decide that its sole function is to compensate, with punishment hived off to the criminal justice system. The public does not necessarily share their views. Celia Wells, in a study of disaster litigation, notes that bereaved relatives use law for a number of different purposes, including:[20]

venting anger or frustration or both, seeking revenge, demanding compensation and wanting to prevent future tragedies.... A variety of legal institutions can be invoked in the search for satisfaction, a search which appears to go beyond mere compensation and becomes a quest for something like 'truth' or 'justice'.

A long list of cases could be compiled in which litigants have turned to tort law to secure accountability for decision-making after other means of public accountability have failed. Many are large class actions of the type deplored by Fleming. In some the obduracy of government is in issue, with 'victims' invoking law for its supposed independence and impartiality. Law is also useful as a publicity vehicle and 'tin opener' when political action seems blocked.[21] A group of claims brought recently against the British Ministry of Defence in respect of the alleged rape of women by British soldiers stationed in Kenya shows how, without the support of the home government, the help of foreign lawyers, and

---

[19] *The Times*, 22 December 2003.
[20] C. Wells, *Negotiating Tragedy: Law and Disasters* (London: Sweet and Maxwell, 1995) at158.
[21] For the use of law in campaigning, see C. Harlow and R. W. Rawlings, *Pressure Through Law* (London: Routledge, 1992).

the backing of the international press, claims from disadvantaged victims are liable to sink without trace.[22]

Twenty years after the Bhopal disaster, there has been no real redress. The 'desultory settlement' negotiated by the Indian government with Union Carbide in respect of claims totalling $3.3 billion produced a fund of $470 million, amounting to $320 per injured victim and $1,430 for the 8,000 dead, much of which has never been received by the beneficiaries. And there has been no true accountability process. Victims' groups have returned to law in desperation, invoking the criminal law, although attempts to charge the chairman of the Union Carbide Board and have him extradited are currently stalled, allegedly through the intervention of the Indian government. Alongside, a class action is under way in New York based on failure of UCC to clear up the site, said to have degenerated into a 'toxic dump', emitting carcinogenic chemicals into the drinking water.[23] We see how support of the home government is easily bought off by pressure from multinational corporations or from powerful foreign governments, which may also intervene to block action against multinationals. It is harder still for victims to bring home claims against a foreign government directly.

On the domestic scene, we have had the Hillsborough accident, where poor policing at a football stadium brought a public inquiry,[24] but also tort actions. These had the effect of exposing the tort action as a poor vehicle for accountability and the judge-made law of nervous shock as deeply flawed.[25] The outstanding class action brought by veterans

[22] This case proceeded with the help of a team of lawyers headed by Martin Day, a British firm experienced in class actions. It was widely publicized by the media. But see the *Daily Telegraph*, 2 October 2003, 14, for the suggestion that the claims were largely fraudulent. The case was later settled.

[23] *Socialist Lawyer*, June 2003 at 22–3.

[24] *Final Report of the Popplewell Inquiry into the Hillsborough Disaster*, Cmnd 9710 (1986)

[25] In *Alcock v Chief Constable of S. Yorkshire Police* [1991] 3 WLR 1057, relatives of the deceased failed in actions for psychiatric damage; in *Frost v Chief Constable of S. Yorkshire Police* [1998] QB254, police officers involved in rescue work succeeded in the Court of Appeal, on the ground

of the Gulf War against the UK government and Ministry of Defence, which systematically refuse to accept the existence of the medical condition known by the victims as 'Gulf Syndrome', has as one of its objectives discovery of medical reports prepared for the Ministry. A key purpose of tort litigation in the Camelford affair, where large-scale contamination of domestic water supplies, due to a leak of aluminium into a reservoir, caused inexplicable illness to those served by a certain reservoir, was simply to get an explanation. Without information, victims felt that there had been no true accountability and, perhaps more important, no guarantee that the water authority had embarked on a successful cleaning up operation. Emphasizing their view of tort law as punitive, however, claimants in the Camelford affair boldly, though ultimately without success,[26] demanded exemplary damages. In all these cases, tort law was, in Linden's famous metaphor,[27] taking on the role of 'ombudsman', demanding answers and compelling actors to justify their actions. For pressure groups and crusading lawyers hoping to open up dark and windowless areas of public administration, tort law is a useful 'tin-opener'. But cases of this type sit uneasily inside the corrective justice model and raise wide questions about the crusading use of tort law. What is the relationship of tort law with accountability? Does accountability, as Oliver has suggested,[28]

of employer's duty of care, an inequity ironed out by the House of Lords; see [1999] 2AC 455. And see Law Commission, *Liability for Psychiatric Illness*, Law Com No 137 (1995) and No 249 (1998) noted by Teff, 'Liability for Psychiatric Illness: Advancing Cautiously' (1999) 61 *MLR* 849.

[26] *AB v South West Water Services* [1993] 1 All ER 609. The point of law raised was whether a public authority could be vicariously liable for exemplary damages in a case based on negligence: see now Law Commission, *Aggravated, Exemplary and Restitutionary Damages*, Law Com No 247 (1997). But see now below at 131.

[27] A. Linden, 'Tort Law as Ombudsman' (1973) 51 *Can. Bar Rev.* 155.

[28] D. Oliver, *Government in the United Kingdom: The Search for Accountability, Effectiveness and Citizenship* (Milton Keynes: Open University Press, 1991) defines accountability (emphasis mine) at 22–8 as 'being liable to be required to give an account or explanation of actions and, where appropriate, to suffer the consequences, take the blame or *undertake to put matters right* if it should appear that errors have been made'. In

necessarily contain an 'amendatory' element? Or have we succumbed to the influence of globalized consumerism and bought the idea that, without financial compensation, accountability is necessarily incomplete?

Many mass tort cases are only remotely connected with individuals, being fought by campaigning groups for their own political purposes. Typical is the round-the-world tobacco litigation, which has escalated into a 'smoking war', aimed not so much at compensation as designed to put the tobacco industry out of business.[29] This campaign joins public and private actors, gunning for industrial concerns but also for government, public authorities, and regulators, seen as complicit in or at least permissive of a state of affairs in which damage is caused. The outcome of the English *McTear* case[30] is, for instance, apparently awaited eagerly by lawyers around Europe, hoping to bring actions of their own. Product liability cases pressurize producers directly, but indirect pressure can also be brought to bear on employers, persuadable through litigation or the threat of litigation to ban smoking as a measure of health and safety in the workplace. The ultimate target is government as regulator or, in the case of the European Union, the sympathetic European Commission.[31] Regulation may in turn trigger compensation claims from producers.[32] Government may itself decide to play the litigation game, as in a case brought by the US government claiming compensation against the tobacco industry for tobacco-related medical costs, with

other words, accountability is both explanatory and amendatory: note, however, that damages are not specified.

[29] S. Sugarman, 'The Smoking War and the Role of Tort', in Cane and Stapleton, above note 2.

[30] *Margaret McTear v Imperial Tobacco*; see for updates www.ashscotland.org.uk

[31] Case C–376/198 *Germany v European Parliament and Commission* [2000] ECR I–8419, where tobacco companies joined Germany to challenge the legality of EU regulation of tobacco advertising.

[32] Case C–319/96 *Brinckmann Tabakfabriken v Skatteministeriet* [1998] ECR I–5255, where compensation was sought for a misinterpretation by Denmark of the EC tax regulations. See also CE 28 Feb 1992 *Arizona Tobacco Products* [1992] Rec 78, an action for compensation in the French courts.

the stated deterrent motive of requiring the industry to change its behaviour.[33] Government is alleging a conspiracy by the industry to deceive and defraud the public concerning the health risks of smoking. Yet if this allegation is true, is government not complicit? And why has governmental power not been used to outlaw the dangerous practice? The campaigning use of tort for political purposes rebounds on the legal system, inviting the expansion of tort law beyond its logical boundaries.

## RESPONSIBILITY AND LIABILITY

In thinking more deeply about issues currently assuming great importance on the international scene, it is helpful to revisit a lecture entitled 'Accountability and Liability', given by Judge Rosalyn Higgins in 1993.[34] Although her title links accountability with *liability*—related ideas that are not identical twins—Higgins actually focuses on *responsibility*, connecting accountability with *moral* responsibility. Like those legal philosophers who link tort law to moral responsibility,[35] Higgins presents international law as a set of *ethical* principles, permitting the objective evaluation of human behaviour and measurement of its resulting consequences against moral standards embedded in law. In European legal systems, the ethical element in liability is normally supplied by the notion of fault. Recently, however, international law has shown itself ready to

[33] *US v Philip Morris Inc.* 116 F Supp 2d 131(DDC 2000), 156 F Supp 2d 1 (DDC 2001). The claim, brought under the Racketeer Influence and Corrupt Organizations Law 18 USC para 1962 is for $289 billion. It has currently reached the stage of transnational litigation over discovery of internal documents: see *BAT v Cowell* (2002) VSCA 197 (Victoria); *US v Philip Morris and BAT (Investments)* 2003 EWCA Civ 3028 (UK).

[34] R. Higgins, *Problems and Process, International Law and How We Use It* (Oxford: Clarendon, 1994), ch. 9 (The Hague Lectures on public international law). The Lectures antedate Lady Higgins' appointment as a judge of the International Court of Justice.

[35] Owen, 'Tort as Blame', 26 *Georgia L Rev.* 703 (1992) at note 68. See also P. Cane, *Responsibility in Law and Morality* (Oxford: Hart Publishing, 2002).

jettison fault,[36] a position cautiously adopted by Higgins, who discusses the 'growing contemporary tendency for certain categories of obligations to entail "strict liability"—that is to say responsibility by reference to events'.[37] This is the 'objective responsibility' of international law. In assessing objective responsibility, the *act* rather than the *actor's conduct* is important or, to put this differently, responsibility is based on *outcome* rather than *input*. For Higgins, the prevention of harm is an 'absolute duty' for the state[38] and it is 'the violation of international law that engages responsibility, without any fault other than the violation itself being necessary'.[39] In private law, this reflects the move from liability for fault or negligence towards strict liability; in public law, we have arrived at the blurring of the crucial lawful/unlawful distinction that is so problematic for state liability.

It is significant that Higgins portrays international law as a normative system but not a system of *rules*.[40] And although she states that the consequence of state responsibility is always in principle reparation,[41] we should note her criticism of the International Law Commission for its emphasis on the remedial toolkit.[42] While tort law deals in liability and provides a remedy in damages, classical international law does not. It deals in responsibility and reparation of a kind that does not always entail financial compensation for *individuals*. Four main categories of redress are recognized in international law: restitution in kind, compensation, satisfaction, and assurances and guarantees against repetition.[43] Here reparation is a matter of

---

[36] J. Crawford, *The International Law Commission's Articles on State Responsibility* (Cambridge: Cambridge University Press, 2002) at 12, discussing Art I of Chap 1 of Part I of the ILC draft of 1996.

[37] Higgins, above note 34, at 161.

[38] At 164–5.

[39] At 160.

[40] At 1.

[41] At 162, citing the *Chorzow* case (1928) PCIJ Ser A, no 17, at 29.

[42] At 164–5.

[43] Crawford, above note 36, at 7, describing the *acquis* of the 1996 ILC draft.

inter-state election and monetary awards to individuals are not necessarily contemplated. On the other hand, Article 2(3) of the Covenant on Civil and Political Rights requires states parties to provide effective and enforceable remedies and imposes an express obligation where possible to devise judicial remedies for individuals. The Van Boven Report on gross violation of human rights, prepared for the United Nations in 1989, provides that:[44]

Reparation shall render justice by removing or redressing the consequences of the wrongful acts and by preventing and deterring violations. Reparations shall be proportionate to the gravity of the violations and the resulting damage and shall include restitution, compensation, rehabilitation, satisfaction and guarantees of non-repetition.

The equivocal position is reflected in the *Lagrand* case,[45] where Germany complained of a failure to notify the consulate of the detention of a German national by a state government of the United States. The US government offered an apology and ultimately took steps to prevent a recurrence and it would seem that compensation for the detainee was not in issue. Where inter-state awards of compensation are forthcoming in respect of injury to individuals, it is probably assumed that appropriate machinery for disbursement to individuals will be established, akin to the machinery of the British Foreign Compensation Acts of 1950 and 1969. Nevertheless, the Van Boven Report may be seen to mark the end of an era and a changed direction in respect of the compensation of individuals in international law.

The trend to individual remedies is not welcomed by everyone. Discussing the ILC proposals at a conference, Tomuschat highlighted the grave risk of backlash or

---

[44] In 1962, the ILC was mandated to produce a 'definition of the general rules governing the international responsibility of the state' in the areas of human rights, disarmament, environmental protection, and law of the sea. The study was completed by T. van Boven, *Study concerning the right to restitution, compensation and rehabilitation for victims of gross violations of human rights and fundamental freedoms: Final Report*, UN Doc E/CN. 4 Sub.2/1993/8, 2 July 1993 at 2.

[45] *Lagrand (Germany v USA)*, judgment of 27 June 2001.

'freezing effect'.[46] On the same occasion, a successful complaint made by a Dutch woman to the UN Human Rights Committee concerning discrimination in the social security system was cited. The Dutch government 'made a quick calculation of the compensation it might by court order be obliged to pay to all potential victims of that discriminatory legal provision and came to the conclusion that this would amount to an enormous sum'. It then seriously considered abrogating, and immediately re-signing, the Convention, this time with a reservation on the discrimination article.[47] States may take their vengeance further, using treaty reservations to protect domestic values and institutions. Ultimately, this could prove a barrier to further human rights conventions—it has indeed been stated that there is already significant resistance by states to provisions in treaties that provide an automatic dispute settlement process on the international level. To date, however, lesser procedural reservations are commoner. These include reservations to remove issues from the justiciability of international jurisdictions and moves to make their decisions advisory rather than binding.[48] Examples of both techniques will be found in the next two sections.

### LIABILITY, SANCTION, AND THE ECJ

Understanding this set of relationships helps to explain and justify the giant step taken by the European Court of Justice in its seminal *Francovich* decision,[49] where liability was imposed on the Member States of the European

---

[46] C. Tomuschat, 'Individual Reparation Claims in Instances of Grave Violations of Human Rights: The Position under General International Law', in A. Randelzhofer and C. Tomuschat (eds), *State Responsibility and the Individual: Reparation in Instances of Grave Violations of Human Rights* (The Hague: Martinus Nijhoff, 1999) at 20–1.

[47] Ibid., at 135 (intervention by Dr Kooimans).

[48] S. Bunn Livingstone, *Juricultural Pluralism vis-à-vis Treaty Law* (Dordrecht: Martinus Nijhoff, 2002) at 297–300.

[49] Joined Cases 6, 9/90 *Francovich and Bonafaci v Italy* [1991] ECR I–5357.

Community for losses caused through failure correctly to implement EC law. No adequate theoretical basis for this brave—or reckless—decision has ever been clearly articulated.[50] All that the ECJ said was that where a Member State failed in its obligation to implement a Community directive, there could be liability provided that:

(i) the directive was intended to confer rights on individuals;

(ii) the content of the rights was clearly spelt out in the directive; and

(iii) a causal link existed between the failure to implement the directive and the loss suffered.

This formulation is entirely compatible with and indeed reflects the conception of strict state responsibility as advocated by Higgins.

I have on an earlier occasion advanced a more detailed argument to the effect that the imposition of *Francovich* liability represents a sanction theory of tort law,[51] in which liability is seen as a substitute for the more intrusive mandatory or punitive remedies not at the time in the possession of the ECJ. What *Francovich* added to the toolkit of the ECJ was the power of sanction. Despite the rhetoric of citizen empowerment in the literature,[52] the expert commentators are united in admitting this: van Gerven[53] refers to liability as a 'sanction, within the framework of the specific Community rule that it purports to make effective', while Caranta more cynically observes that 'effective

---

[50] The enormous literature is conveniently listed by R. Caranta, 'Judicial Protection Against Member States: A New *Jus Commune* Takes Shape' (1995) 32 *CML Rev.* 703 at note 24.

[51] C. Harlow, 'Francovich and the Problem of the Disobedient State' (1996) 2 *ELJ* 199, 204–10.

[52] E. Szyszczak, 'Making Europe More Relevant to its Citizens' (1996) 21 *EL Rev.* 35; J. Steiner, 'From Direct Effects to *Francovich*: Shifting Means of Enforcement of Community Law' (1993) 18 *EL Rev.* 3.

[53] W. Van Gerven, 'Bridging the Gap Between Community and National Laws: Towards a Principle of Homogeneity in the Field of Legal Remedies?' (1995) 32 *CML Rev.* 679, 694. See also F. Schockweiler, 'La responsabilité de l'autorité nationale en cas de violation du droit communautaire' (1992) 28 *RTDE* 27, 42.

judicial protection' is used 'more to exact obedience from
Member States than to protect citizens'.[54] There are latent
references here to a second strand in the Court's thinking at
this period, that individuals—or more usually, private commercial corporations—could be mobilized as a 'private
police force' and play a central part in the enforcement of
Community law. This then was the unsympathetic context
in which the ECJ embarked on the path of Member State
liability.

*Francovich* must then be seen as an assertion of power or
even act of defiance by the ECJ—it was certainly not a step
taken at the behest of the Member States. Amongst academics, however, the new doctrine generally received an enthu-
siastic welcome, lending strength to a wider campaign for a
general harmonization of European tort law. Van Gerven,
for example, positively celebrates the novelty of the *Francovich* principle, as a break with the previously accepted
rule that EC law was not designed to create new remedies
in the national courts to ensure the observance of Community law other than those already laid down by national
law.[55] He concludes that, after *Francovich*, Member States
must, at the very least, *broaden* existing remedies.[56] But is
the *Francovich* principle 'novel', as asserted by van Gerven,
or is it a prime example of the 'cascade effect'? An easy
precedent for Member State liability did exist; it is to be
found in the so-called '*Schöppenstedt* formula' of Community law,[57] applicable to the liability of the Community for
loss caused by regulatory or legislative measures involving
choices of economic policy. In these circumstances,
according to the *Schöppenstedt* formula, the EU institutions
incur liability only where there has been:

---

[54] Caranta, above note 50, at 710.
[55] W. van Gerven, 'Non-contractual Liability of Member States, Community Institutions and Individuals for Breaches of Community Law
with a View to a Common Law for Europe' (1994) 1 *Maastricht J of
Comp. Law* 6.
[56] Van Gerven, above note 53, at 693.
[57] Case 5/71 *Zuckerfabrik Schöppenstedt v Council* [1971] ECR 975. See
for discussion, T. C. Hartley, *The Foundations of European Community Law*
(4th edn, Oxford: Clarendon, 1998) at 465–76.

(i)   a sufficiently serious breach of
(ii)  a superior rule of law
(iii) designed for the protection of the individual.

Since this formulation is taken from case law rather than the Treaties, it merely pushes our inquiry one stage further back. The Treaties specifically link Community liability to national legal systems, by providing that the Community and its institutions shall, in making reparation, act 'in accordance with the general principles common to the laws of the Member States'.[58] What these principles actually were and what they had in common must, in light of the fragmentary evidence, remain largely a matter of conjecture. Expert commentators are, however, more or less agreed that by no means all, and perhaps not even a majority of, national legal systems contained a liability principle similar to *Schöppenstedt*.

The likelihood is that *Francovich* reflects a compensation principle borrowed from Germany, though it resembles a similar principle used in French administrative courts. In German law several related principles are available,[59] most relevant being the *Schutznormtheorie*. According to this doctrine, compensation is due to an individual who has suffered loss through:

(i)   a serious violation of
(ii)  a 'superior rule of law'
(iii) intended for the protection of individuals.[60]

---

[58] TEC Art 288 (ex 215) para 2.

[59] Consider also the principles of 'sacrificial encroachment' (*Aufopferung*) and expropriation (*Enteignung*). An outline of German law is provided in W. Rüfner, 'Basic Elements of German Law on State Liability' in J. Bell and A. Bradley (eds), *Governmental Liability: A Comparative Study* (London: UK National Committee of Comparative Law, 1991). See also W. Van Gerven, 'Bridging the Unbridgeable: Community and National Tort Laws after *Francovich* and *Brasserie*' (1996) 45 *ICLQ* 507.

[60] *Schutznormtheorie* is defined by E. Grabitz, 'Liability for Legislative Acts' in H. Schermers, T. Heukels, and P. Mead (eds), *Non-contractual Liability of the European Communities* (Dordrecht: Martinus Nijhoff, 1988) at 6, to mean that 'the state is liable only when, in addition to causing an injury, it breaches a *Schutznorm* or legal norm protecting a subjective public right of the injured party and which is intended not only to protect

This principle, similar to *Schöppenstedt*, merits further reflection in the context of my subject, as it is clearly capable of linking state liability to international human rights. Note, however, that *compensation* rather than *liability* seems to be in issue.

In French administrative law, a somewhat similar compensation principle, based on the concept of 'equality before public charges' (*égalité devant les charges publiques*), is recognized. The equality principle is not the general principle of administrative liability in France: that place is reserved for fault. Reflecting an ethos of social solidarity and collective responsibility,[61] it provides a basis for compensation in a few exceptional cases. Underlying the principle is the belief that citizens are entitled to correct application of the law and to an acceptable standard of public services. When the state fails to carry out its obligations it is normally deemed to be at fault,[62] but in circumstances where the state is able to show that it has acted legally and properly, the equality principle can be invoked as a basis for compensation.[63] Later case law has tentatively extended the doctrine to legislative measures laying excessive burdens on particular individuals or sections of the community—a wide principle, which could easily engulf the entire system of state liability but has never been permitted to do so.[64] The French Conseil d'Etat, which

individuals in general but also to protect a *specific circle* of individuals to which the injured party belongs'. In Joined Cases 5 & 7, 13–24/66 *Kampffmeyer v Commission* [1967] ECR 245, however, the ECJ ruled that it can be enough for liability if the protection is for individuals *generally*.

[61] See the discussion in the Introduction to these lectures at note 7.

[62] The formulation employed is usually the ambiguous formula of 'fault of such a nature as to entail liability' or '*faute caracterisée*': see for further explanation D. Fairgrieve, *State Liability in Tort* (Oxford: Oxford University Press, 2002) at 106–22.

[63] CE 30 November 1923 *Couitéas* [1923] Rec. 789; M. Long *et al.*, *Grands Arrêts de la jurisprudence administrative* (10th edn, Paris: Sirey, 1993) No. 45. The principle is thought to derive from Art 13 of the Declaration of the Rights of Man of 26 August 1789, where it referred to taxes: Errera, 'The Scope and Meaning of No-Fault Liability in French Administrative Law' [1986] *Current Legal Problems* 157.

[64] CE Ass 14 January 1938 *Sté Anonyme des Produits Laitiers 'La Fleurette'* [1938] Rec. 25 or note under GA No 58. For development and

introduced the principle, has subsequently reserved it for exceptional 'hard cases' not covered by existing liability principles and has imposed strict control devices, in particular by restricting compensation to 'abnormal losses'. In France then, this doctrine applies only in exceptional circumstances and is generally accepted to be an *equitable* remedy.[65]

What the two doctrines have in common is that they are not, in their inception, *liability* principles—in every European system fault still holds primacy in this respect—but *compensation* principles covering only exceptional cases. As general principles of liability, they would be dangerous because they break the crucial link between fault, illegality, and liability. Because they are not fault-based, they are easily capable of extension to cover lawful administrative acts and action; this is, indeed, the very reason why they were created and why they have been expounded as principles of *compensation* and not of liability. This is a distinction of importance, picked up in my final lecture, where I shall argue that we should retain the tradition of reserving questions of compensation for the political authorities and a non-legal process.

Absorbed into the Community legal system, these compensation principles are intentionally expansive, their very purpose being to introduce liability into situations where no liability previously existed. But they have a wider indirect impact, affecting national legal systems in unexpected ways. As the doctrines have been transplanted, their coherence has been diluted by the removal of internal control devices.[66] Thus the French equality doctrine was reined in by the requirement of 'abnormal loss'; this criterion for

'constitutionalization' of the equality principle in French law, see Gohin, 'La responsibilité de l'état en tant que legislateur' [1998] *RIDC* 595.

[65] J-P. Gilli, 'La responsibilité de la puissance publique' *D* 1971 chr 125; Debard, 'L'égalité des citoyens devant les charges publiques; fondement incertain de la responsibilité administrative' *D* 1987 Chr 158; G. Pelissier, *Le principe d'egalité en droit public* (Paris: 1996).

[66] The effects of transplant into national systems are considered by Van Gerven, 'Bridging the Gap', above note 53.

liability was thrown into doubt by the EC intruder.[67] And *Francovich* has been particularly hard to reconcile with the common law system, where the doctrine sits uneasily inside the law of torts, defying classification as a breach of statutory duty.[68] When, as in the notorious *Factortame* case,[69] this term is used to describe liability for loss flowing directly from an Act of Parliament, it is nothing less than a constitutional enormity!

What we are seeing is a globalized variant of the 'selective comparison' process described in the context of the domestic tort law system by Atiyah,[70] whereby courts are persuaded or, in the instant case, compelled to ratchet up their liability system by reference to foreign legal systems or the practice of foreign courts, often, it has to be said, imperfectly understood. For functionalists, this inevitably raises the question: is Member State liability really necessary? Are the problems of non-implementation serious enough to warrant the nuclear sanction of state liability? Or is the true issue the status and standing of certain courts? Liability is, after all, a highly intrusive remedy, with considerable impact on national constitutions. Relationships between national governments and constituent regional authorities are complex. Regional authorities are frequently invested with a considerable degree of autonomy, making it difficult for the state to ensure compliance. Even transposition may require the co-operation of regional legislatures, while enforcement and compliance are often regional or even local responsibilities. These relationships are thrown out of kilter

[67] On the national application of EC state liability law, see CE Ass 28 February 1992 *Arizona Tobacco Products* [1992] Rec. 78 and CAA Paris 1 July 1992 *Dangeville* [1992] Rec. 558; CE Ass 30 October 1996 *Dangeville* [1996] Rec. 399. And see Van Gerven, above note 53, at 536–7.

[68] Convery, 'State Liability in the UK after *Brasserie du Pêcheur*' (1997) 34 *CML Rev.* 603; M. Hoskins, 'Rebirth of the Innominate Tort?' in J. Beatson and T. Tridimas (eds), *New Directions in European Public Law* (Oxford: Hart Publishing, 1998).

[69] Case C–213/89 *R v Secretary of State for Transport ex p Factortame (No 2)* [1990] ECR I–2433; *R v Secretary of State for Transport ex p Factortame (No 3)* [1992] 3 WLR 288.

[70] P. Atiyah, *The Damages Lottery* (Oxford: Hart Publishing, 1997).

by the rules of Community law that place the twin duties of compliance and compensation on the Member State.[71] The practice in more developed federal systems is notably less intrusive; in the United States, for example, federal and state authorities are not encouraged to settle their differences in court.[72] We should not forget too that, where the state is involved, the liability judgment may itself prove unenforceable.

The Commission's annual reports boast of a consistently high level of implementation, though there are undoubtedly intractable cases.[73] The scheme established by the Treaties requires the Commission to sort these out, largely by recourse to diplomatic methods.[74] And the case for state liability is now greatly reduced by the introduction of the 'penalty payment' procedure, agreed directly after *Francovich* at the Maastricht IGC, where a new power was added to

---

[71] In Case C–302/97 *Klaus Könle v Republic of Austria* [1999] ECRI–3099 the validity of a Tyrolese law advantaging Austrian nationals procedurally in the land registration system was challenged. Although the ECJ stated firmly that 'Community law does not require Member States to make any change in the distribution of powers and responsibilities between the public bodies which exist on their territory', the Member State could not rely on inability to enforce the law as a defence against liability.

[72] J. Pfander, 'Member State Liability and Constitutional Change in the United States and Europe' (2003) 51 *AJCL* 237 contrasts the two systems, citing *Seminole Tribe v Florida* 517 US 44 (1996); *Alden v Maine* 527 US 706 (1999); *Florida Prepaid Postsecondary Education Expense Board v College Savings Bank* 527 US 627 (1999); and *College Savings Bank v Florida Prepaid Postsecondary Education Expense Board* 527 US 666 (1999), which set in place rules of immunity.

[73] Over 90% of European Union directives are reported annually by the Commission in its Scoreboard as having been transposed. In December 2000, the Commission reported 25 judgments as temporarily not implemented, in six of which Art 228 proceedings (below) were threatened. But see C. Harding, 'Member State Enforcement of European and Community Measures: The Chimera of Effective Enforcement' (1997) 4 *Maastricht J of Int. and European Law* 5.

[74] F. Snyder, 'The Effectiveness of European Community Law: Institutions, Processes, Tools and Techniques' (1993) 56 *MLR* 19. Compare the argument for 'responsive regulation' advanced by I. Ayres and J. Braithwaite, *Responsive Regulation: Transcending the Regulation Debate* (Oxford: Oxford University Press, 1992).

TEC Article 228 to 'fine' defaulting Member States.[75] This would, if the Draft European Constitution were to be implemented, be heightened and the procedures streamlined.[76] Article 228 procedure was used first against Greece, after the Greek government had failed to implement the EC Waste Directives in respect of a site in Crete operated by a regional authority and used for the disposal of toxic and dangerous waste. The ECJ ruled that Greece was in breach of its obligations; five years later, as no remedial action had been taken, the Commission returned to the Court asking for a penalty payment, and a daily fine of 20,000 euros was duly imposed.[77] But law is not, as lawyers seem to think, self-implementing; resort to negotiation and persuasion remains inevitable and much patient work remained for the Commission. Eighteen months later, when a start had been made at paying the 4.2 million euros owing under threat that the Commission would otherwise begin to withhold aid payments, the offending dump of toxic waste was still in operation.[78] In its judgment in the second case, involving Spain, the ECJ itself admitted in extenuation of Spain that full compliance with the Bathing Water Directives was 'hard to achieve' and

[75] The amendment to TEC Art 228 provides: 'If the Member State concerned fails to take the necessary measures to comply with the Court's judgment within the time-limit laid down by the Commission, the latter may bring the case before the Court of Justice. In so doing it shall specify the amount of the lump sum or penalty payment to be paid by the Member State concerned which it considers appropriate in the circumstances. If the Court of Justice finds that the Member State concerned has not complied with its judgment it may impose a lump sum or penalty payment on it.'

[76] Title VI Art III–265 of the Draft European Constitution replicates TEC Art 226. Art III–267 reforms the present TEC Art 228 by combining the earlier administrative stages of the process and obviating the need for a 'reasoned opinion'. Para 3 obviates the necessity for two separate applications to the ECJ, allowing the Commission at its discretion to request a penalty payment in proceedings against a Member State in respect of failures to notify the Commission of transposition.

[77] Case C–45/91 *Commission v Greece* [1992] ECR I–2509; Case C–387/97 *Commission v Greece* [2000] ECR I–5047.

[78] See, further, M. Theodossiou, 'An Analysis of the Recent Response of the Community to Non-compliance with Court of Justice Judgments: Article 228(2) EC' (2002) 27 *EL Rev*. 25.

'involved complex operations'.[79] It might have added that many other Member States were in default.

The very real problems involved in implementation are tacitly acknowledged by the new EU regime of environmental liability. This has departed radically from the classical civil liability model and has, according to one commentator, been transmuted into a vehicle for protecting aggregative interests:[80]

It is now a public law regime, where damage to biodiversity, water resources and site contamination is to be cleared up as a matter of public interest and where the regime is regulated by competent authorities. Personal injuries and damages to health are excluded from a regime concerned solely with damage to the environment. In addition, the proposal makes it clear that the Directive is not to 'give all parties a right of compensation for any economic losses they may have incurred'.

'Whiplash effect' is another phenomenon often overlooked by lawyers, who tend to downplay the generally hostile response to *Francovich*. Reaction from national courts to *Francovich* liability has been said to range from 'hesitancy and reluctance' to cases of near 'emasculation'.[81] In Italy the judgment temporarily put in issue the doctrine of supremacy,[82] while the claimants in *Francovich* and *Brasserie*, after protracted further litigation, finally obtained no compensation. There was too serious political backlash from Member State governments with reactions ranging

---

[79] Case C–278/01 *Commission v Spain* (judgment of 25 November 2003).

[80] Thornton, 'Environmental Liability—a Shrinking Mirage or the Most Realistic Attempt So Far?' [2003] *JPEL* 272, 274. One should not deduce that individual actions for economic and other loss will be wholly excluded but they will not be covered by the proposed directive.

[81] J. Talberg, 'Supranational Influence in EU Enforcement: the ECJ and the Principle of State Liability' (2000) 7 *JEPP* 104 at 116, 117. It must be remembered that the ECJ is restricted to advising on points of EC law: success or failure in the substantive action remains a question for the national court. The UK appears to be an exception to the reluctance noted in the text, embracing the liability principle enthusiastically and dutifully applying it in the *Factortame* case: *R v Secretary of State for Transport ex p Factortame (No 5)* [1999] 3 WLR 1062 (Lord Slynn).

[82] Cas civ sez lavoro 11 October 1995 n. 10617 noted *Danno e Responsibilità* January/February 1996 at 78.

from Germany's attempt to curtail the ambit of the Court's jurisdiction to an ultimately unsuccessful UK proposal at the pre-Maastricht IGC both to limit state liability and to curtail the retrospective effect of ECJ judgments.[83] Although the ECJ finally emerged unscathed, its wings were clipped by the same Treaty in the area of Justice and Home Affairs.[84]

Tomuschat has attributed the ECJ decision not to rule that WTO and GATT rulings were directly enforceable within the Community to its premonition that the Community might thereby be exposed to financially crippling reparation actions.[85] His point receives support from the recent *Biret* action,[86] where the biter nearly found itself bitten. Biret, a French food importer, claimed reparation from the Community for loss flowing from a Council Directive prohibiting import into the EU of meat treated with hormones, contrary to a ruling from the WTO dispute settlement body. This claim was abruptly dismissed by the CFI, on the ground that the WTO Agreement was not directly effective. On appeal to the ECJ, however, the Advocate-General wanted the issue of liability to be re-opened, advising, on the basis of *Francovich*, that, at least for purposes of compensation, the Agreement had direct effect. This proved to be, however, one of the rare cases in which

---

[83] Talberg, above note 81, at 114–15.

[84] TEC Art 68. For detailed exposition see S. Peers, 'Who's Judging the Watchmen? The Judicial System of the Area of Freedom and Justice' [2000] *YEL* 237. For the suggestion that the Court's subsequent case law has become more deferential see E. Guild and S. Peers, 'Deference or Defiance? The Court of Justice's Jurisdiction in Immigration and Asylum' in E. Guild and C. Harlow (eds), *Implementing Amsterdam, Immigration and Asylum rights in EC Law* (Oxford: Hart Publishing, 2000) at 274.

[85] C. Tomuschat, 'Individual Reparation Claims in Instances of Grave Human Rights Violations: the Position under General International Law' in A. Randelzhofer and C. Tomuschat (eds), *State Responsibility and the Individual: Reparation in Instances of Grave Violations of Human Rights* (The Hague: Martinus Nijhoff, 1999) at 9.

[86] Case T–174/01 *Biret International SA v Council* [2002] ECR II–17; Case C–93/02P *Biret International SA v Council*, Case C–94/02 P *Etablissements Biret et Cie SA v Council*, Opinion of Alber A-G, 15 May 2003; judgment of 30 September 2003.

the ECJ failed to follow the recommendations of its Advocate-General.[87]

Fear of whiplash may help to explain why the ECJ has, in recent years, begun to 'reshape the contours' of its liability system. Evidence for retraction has been seen in the more sympathetic attitude to alternative remedies, including a less strict attitude to administrative compensation schemes.[88] This may be partly due to an unhappy experience in the Milk Quotas Saga, following invalidation of EC regulations that restructured the system of milk premiums and introduced a new quota system.[89] Confusion followed, opening the proverbial floodgate and bringing a caseload that allegedly led to a transfer of competence to the CFI. Perhaps this brought the realization that multiple claims often lie behind liability judgments and that these can, with the best will in the world, cause serious logistical problems for those who have to implement them. In the Milk Quotas cases, the regulations setting up the compensation scheme were themselves successfully challenged. For the first time, the Court authorized a scheme based on a flat rate offer, subject only to the provision that acceptance is optional, thus leaving the right to litigate open.[90] Can we hear a distant echo of asbestos?

[87] Despite the fact that, in Case C–352/98 P, *Laboratoires Pharmaceutiques Bergaderm and Goupil v Commission* [2000] ECR-I-5291, the ECJ had ruled that liability of Member States under *Francovich* and of the Community and its institutions under the *Schöppenstedt* formula was to be considered commensurate.

[88] M. Dougan, 'The Francovich Right to Reparation: Reshaping the Contours of Community Remedial Competence' (2000) 6 *European Public Law* 103.

[89] Council Regulations 1078/77 [1977] OJ L131/1 and 856/84 [1984] OJ L90 and 857/84, invalidated by Case 120/86 *Mulder I* [1988] ECR 2321 and Case 170/86 *Von Deetzen* [1988] ECR 2355. Case C–104/89 *Mulder II* [1992] ECR I–3061, noted by T. Heukels (1993) 30 *CML Rev.* 368 and by W. Van Gerven, (1994) 1 *Maastricht J of Comp. Law* 6, provided for compensation by the Community.

[90] In Case T–541/193, *Connaughton v Council* [1997] ECR II–549; Case T–554/93 *Saint and Murray v Council and Commission* [1997] ECR II–563; Case T–2094 *Hartmann v Council and Commission* [1997] ECR II–595, noted by Cardwell (1998) 35 *CML Rev.* 971. Cardwell estimates that around

### THE STRASBOURG COURT AND SATISFACTION:
### JUST OR UNJUST?

The European Court of Human Rights is not the usual forum for ordering compensation in respect of human rights violations; that is a question for national courts. In two instances it can, however, intervene more directly: ECHR Article 13 provides that national authorities must provide an effective remedy in cases of violation of human rights,[91] while under ECHR Article 41 (previously Article 50) the ECtHR may, if the state party allows 'only partial reparation', itself 'afford just satisfaction to the injured party'.[92] In both cases, it may then fall to the ECtHR to consider the appropriateness or adequacy of compensation available under national law; in other words, the article apparently envisages a supervisory role for the ECtHR. In addition, ECHR Article 6(1) provides for access, in cases involving a determination of someone's civil rights and obligations, to a court or tribunal. Somewhat unexpectedly, this article, designed to protect access to court, has been found to bite on the substantive rules of liability.

A first stage in the process of expansion occurred when the ECtHR extended its supervisory jurisdiction under then Article 41 by treating a demand for just satisfaction, not as a separate application, but as the final phase in an application for substantive violation. It ruled that Article 41 did not call for exhaustion of domestic remedies and that the ECtHR could impose its own order for redress without awaiting an

13,000 farmers claimed milk quotas after *Mulder I* and that 589 applicants actually commenced proceedings.

[91] Art 13 reads: 'Everyone whose rights and freedoms as set forth in this Convention are violated shall have an effective remedy before a national authority notwithstanding that the violation has been committed by persons acting in an official capacity'.

[92] Art 41 reads: 'If the Court finds that there has been a violation of the Convention or the protocols thereto, and if the internal law of the High Contracting party concerned allows only partial reparation to be made, the Court shall, if necessary, afford just satisfaction to the injured party'.

offer of compensation from the national government.[93] This ruling was intended to obviate the need for multiple applications to the Court. Effectively, however, it set up an application to the ECtHR as an alternative in some cases to a claim for damages in a national court, a position providing the ECtHR with opportunities for intervention that have been taken up in some of the recent cases. In the same judgment, the ECtHR affirmed as its basic principle of compensation the familiar legal rule of full restitution (*restitutio in integrum*). Even more significantly, it established the unrelated point that 'in questions of liability arising from the failure to observe the Convention, there is in any event no room to distinguish between acts and omissions'.[94] Not only is this attitude to omissions very different from the line taken by the common law, but it also extends the 'irradiating influence' of human rights to liability, making it possible for the state to be held responsible for violations of human rights for which private actors could not necessarily be found liable. As in those modern tort cases where the substitution of a peripheral party for the primary actor is permitted,[95] the liability of the state then stands as a substitute for or guarantor of the direct application of human rights documents to private parties, giving them an indirect 'horizontal effect'.[96]

Nevertheless, for many years the approach of the ECtHR to the reparation provisions was restrained. As with the international law system from which Convention law derives, the ECtHR was open-minded with regard to redress and reparation. It was prepared to take into account all the measures that a state might in international law reasonably

---

[93] *De Wilde, Ooms and Versyp v Belgium (No 2)* (1972) 1 EHRR 438. There are strongly reasoned dissenting judgments on this point, notably from Judge Verdross (at para 4), who thought that it would be 'in accordance with the spirit and general system of the Convention for the Court first to allow the respondent State the option of granting the injured party adequate compensation by its own procedure'.

[94] At para 22.

[95] See Chap. 1, text at note 45.

[96] For explanation see Hunt, 'The 'Horizontal Effect of the Human Rights Act' [1998] *PL* 423.

be expected to take in respect of a violation: apology, punishment of responsible individuals, the taking of steps to prevent recurrence, restitution, and other forms of just satisfaction. The emphasis was less on enriching individuals than on standard setting, the priority being to establish, publicize, and to see human rights standards brought into effect.[97] The Council of Europe dealt in *political* outcomes, the political character of its machinery being emphasized by the fact that it was originally left to the Committee of Ministers or 'concerned states' to decide whether or not the judicial process would even be invoked.[98] Similarly, the principal machinery for rectification of violations and enforcement of the Court's judgments was—and remains today—the Committee of Ministers, which exercises a supervisory function in such matters.[99]

In the scheme as originally devised, the Commission on Human Rights formed an important bridge to 'friendly settlement' of cases that seemed likely to pass the threshold of admissibility. By standards of domestic law, the resolution might sometimes seem unorthodox, as in the inter-state case of *Denmark v Turkey*,[100] where Denmark complained of an Article 3 violation in respect of a Danish citizen who had been detained and had suffered ill treatment at the hands of the police during a visit to Turkey. The agreed friendly settlement included an *ex gratia* payment for the individual but dwelt primarily on the establishment of a new Council of Europe training programme for police investigators, in which Turkey would participate and to which both Denmark and Turkey would contribute financially. The two countries also agreed to set in place an action plan and a 'continuous bilateral Danish–Turkish political dialogue', within the framework of which allegations of

[97] K. Reid, *A Practitioner's Guide to the ECHR* (London: Sweet and Maxwell, 1998) at 398.

[98] ECHR Arts 32 and 46 amended by Protocol 9 to allow the applicant to refer a case to the Court, now replaced by Protocol 11.

[99] Formerly ECHR Art 54, now Art 46(2).

[100] Application No 34383/97 *Denmark v Turkey* (judgment of 5 April 2000).

torture and ill treatment would in future be raised. On the demise of the Commission, responsibility for supervision of friendly settlement procedure was transferred to the new Court set up by the new ECHR Protocol 11, but it seems that the intention was not to judicialize the procedure. It is now the Court's Registrar who supervises the arrangements, the first incumbent of the office being the last Secretary of the defunct Commission.[101] Whether this transfer will in practice presage judicialization remains to be seen.

Historically, when money awards were under consideration, the ECtHR adopted 'an equitable case-by-case approach'. All that was clear was that, as indicated above, the ECtHR worked on the principle of *restitutio in integrum* and that the possibility of exemplary damages was firmly excluded.[102] Otherwise the ECtHR focused on the facts of individual cases, often without reference to apparently similar rulings; the Court seemed to see itself as an ombudsman or mediator recommending compensation, rather than as a court deciding liability and calculating damages. As with the French Conseil d'Etat and the equality principle, its jurisdiction possessed the character of a residual equitable jurisdiction, reserved for exceptional or 'abnormal' cases. The effect, in the opinion of the English Law Commission, was to introduce 'apparently irreconcilable inconsistencies'.[103]

But with the unfortunate *Osman* case[104]—an object lesson to government lawyers not to fight questions of principle on unfavourable facts—the ECtHR moved into expansive

---

[101] The original procedure is described in Kruger and Norgaard, 'Reflections Concerning Friendly Settlement under the ECHR' in F. Matscher and H. Petzold (eds), *Protecting Human Rights: The European Dimension* (Cologne: C. Heymann, 1988). See Art 48 of Protocol 11 for the new arrangements, noted by A. Mowbray, 'Reform of the Control System of the European Convention on Human Rights' [1993] *PL* 419. Flesh is put on the bones by A. Mowbray, *Cases and Materials on the European Convention on Human Rights* (London: Butterworths, 2001) at 16–27.

[102] *Aksoy v Turkey* (1996) 23 EHRR 553. (In a case of torture, compensatory damages of £324,325 were awarded but neither punitive nor aggravated damages were available.)

[103] Law Commission, *Damages Under The Human Rights Act 1998*, Law Com No 266, Cm 4853 (2000) at para 3.5.

[104] *Osman v United Kingdom* (1998) 29 EHRR 245.

mode. The case centred on the signal failure of the police, though apprised of at least some of the circumstances, to protect a schoolboy from the harassment of an unbalanced teacher. Ahmet Osman had been harassed for around two years by the unwanted attentions of this teacher, who had become increasingly unstable, as evidenced by his involvement in acts of criminal damage, violence, and dangerous driving. He was referred to a psychiatrist, who recommended leave of absence on medical grounds, and finally formally reprimanded by the education authority, despite which he continued to work in the area as a supply teacher. The police laid charges of criminal damage and dangerous driving but unfortunately failed to arrest the man, as he was away from home. The episode culminated in fatal shootings: Ahmet's father was killed and Ahmet seriously injured. The affair was not marked by a high degree of competent and effective management on the part of the authorities, though the precise facts and the extent of police involvement and knowledge were contested by the police and never fully tested either at a criminal or civil trial or at coroner's inquest—itself a demonstrable failure of the machinery for accountability.[105] It is unfortunate too that the appropriate authorities chose to stand on the letter of the law and did not show sufficient common sense and humanity to proffer an appropriate apology and a moderate compensation payment such as an ombudsman would have ordered in a clear case of maladministration. In these circumstances, the only option was a civil action in negligence against both the psychiatrist and the police.[106] These were,

---

[105] The absence of an inquest is explained by the fact that the teacher, Paul Paget-Lewis, pleaded guilty to two counts of manslaughter; a full account is given by L. Hoyano, 'Policing Flawed Police Investigations: Unravelling the Blanket' (1999) 62 *MLR* 912, 913–15. It was perhaps unfortunate too that neither the Commission for Local Administration nor the Parliamentary Commissioner is competent to investigate police investigations and that the Police Complaints Authority, which has jurisdiction in such cases, has no power to award compensation: see C. Harlow and R. W. Rawlings, *Law and Administration* (2nd edn, London: Butterworths, 1997) at 417–19.

[106] *Osman v Ferguson and another* [1993] 4 All ER 344 (CA).

however, struck out. Accountability had once more proved elusive. Tort law had proved an ineffective ombudsman. The lawyers turned to human rights. The case thus ended in the Court of Human Rights at Strasbourg, which ruled that there had been no substantive violation of ECHR Article 2 (right to life). There had on the other hand been a violation of ECHR Article 6(1); by striking out the action, the national courts had deprived the applicants of their right to a judicial hearing. A presumption against liability, treated as contestable in national courts in some specific cases,[107] had thus effectively been converted into a 'blanket immunity' from liability for the police force.

This ruling provoked a barrage of academic and judicial criticism at national level,[108] largely on the ground that the ECtHR had confused a *procedural* right of access to a court, amply met by the full consideration given to the legal issues in the High Court and Court of Appeal, with a *substantive* ruling on the ambit of the tort of negligence in national law and in particular the 'fair, just, and reasonable' test established for negligence by the *Caparo* case.[109] This is a critique with which I broadly agree and which I do not want to revisit. Instead, I want to focus on the concepts of 'access' and 'remedy' towards which the ECtHR seems to be groping and the effect they are likely to have on state liability.

The point of departure for the Court is ECHR Article 6(1), which provides:

---

[107] *Knightley v Johns* [1982] 1 All ER 301; *Kirkham v Chief Constable of Manchester* [1989] 2 QB 283; *Swinney v CC of Northumbria Police Force* [1996] 3 WLR 968. But see also *Alexandrou v Oxford* [1993] 4 All ER 328.

[108] See, for expressions of judicial concern, Lord Browne-Wilkinson in *Barrett v Enfield LBC* [1999] 3 All ER 193, 197; *Kent v Griffiths* [2000] 2 All ER 474, 484 (Lord Woolf CJ); Lord Hoffmann, 'Human Rights and the House of Lords' (1999) 62 *MLR* 159, 164. For academic debate see P. Craig and D. Fairgrieve, 'Barrett, Negligence and Discretionary Powers' [1999] *PL* 626; Murphy, 'Children in Need: the Limits of Local Authority Accountability' (2003) 23 *Legal Studies* 103. And, more generally, see Wright, 'Local Authorities, the Duty of Care and the European Convention on Human Rights' (1998) 18 *OJLS* 1.

[109] *Caparo Industries plc v Dickman* [1990] 1 All ER 568; *Hill v Chief Constable of W. Yorkshire* [1988] 2 All ER 238.

In the determination of his civil rights and obligations or of any criminal charge against him, everyone is entitled to a fair and public hearing within a reasonable time by an independent and impartial tribunal established by law. . . .

In the terminology of the ECtHR, this embodies the 'right to a court'.

It is perhaps hard to maintain that this provision is breached in a case that has received full consideration at the higher levels of the judicial system but, unanimously, the ECtHR in *Osman* found otherwise. By treating the public policy immunity as absolute, the Court reasoned, national courts had ruled out adequate consideration of other public interest considerations that might operate to negative the immunity *on the facts of the specific case*. This is, of course, a considerable extension of the right of *access*. In earlier rulings, however, the ECtHR had got round this obstacle by reasoning that the right to institute proceedings constitutes *'one aspect of'* access. To put this differently, it remains open to the ECtHR to find that 'the *degree* of access' is insufficient to 'secure the individual's right to a court, having regard to the rule of law in a democratic society'.[110]

It might be acceptable that this proviso should entitle the ECtHR to examine whether national *procedural* barriers, such as limitation periods, statutory and judge-made, are justifiable or disproportionate.[111] To extend this scrutiny to the substance of the law[112] is arguably another matter. This was, of course, the interpretation placed on the *Osman* ruling by critical commentators at national level. What

---

[110] *Osman*, above note 104, at para 147, citing *Ashingdane v United Kingdom* (1985) 7 EHRR 528, para 57. The pathway to this conclusion is set out in some detail by C. Gearty, 'Unravelling Osman' (2001) 64 *MLR* 159, 166–9.

[111] *Stubbings and others v United Kingdom* (1996) 23 EHRR 213 (challenging the application of the Limitation Act 1980 to an action in tort in respect of sexual abuse suffered in childhood); *Powell and Rayner v United Kingdom* (1989) 12 EHRR 287 (contesting the validity of s. 76(1) of the Civil Aviation Act 1982, which virtually bars liability in nuisance in civil aviation claims).

[112] *James v United Kingdom* (1986) 8 EHRR 123 (testing the validity of the Leasehold Reform Act 1967, creating a new right in long leaseholders to purchase the freehold).

seemed to them to have happened was a slippage in the Court's reasoning whereby ECHR Article 6(1) had been transformed from a procedural right, 'parasitic' upon the prior existence of an arguable substantive right, into a free-standing right to have one's substantive claim considered. The reply to this argument is that 'access to a court' requires more than the mere assertion by the court that no right to compensation exists; it requires the court also to consider the specific case before it, a process made difficult by the English courts' use of the 'striking out' procedure. If this reasoning is correct, then the main impact of the ECtHR's intervention on liability would be (as noted in my last lecture) that a flood of cases might arise, all of which would need to be set down for trial, leading no doubt to more frequent settlements favourable to claimants.

In *Osman*, the ECtHR made no finding under ECHR Article 13. Instead, dismissing the argument of the UK government that a finding of violation would be enough in itself to constitute 'just satisfaction', the Court used ECHR Article 41 to award 'on an equitable basis' a sum of £10,000 to each of the applicants, essentially for 'loss of a chance' fully to present their case.[113] This outcome is justifiable in the interests of ending an already interminable saga: the affair had already been going on for twelve years. It can also be read as an encouragement and reward to applicants to bring their complaints to Strasbourg.

The later case of *Z v United Kingdom*,[114] concerning the right of children to sue a local authority for negligence in the exercise of its statutory child care functions, is normally read as a retraction and something of an apology by the ECtHR.[115] Not only did the Court sanction the 'striking-out procedure', threatened under the earlier ruling, but it also stated clearly that a finding that no duty of care was owed could not be characterized as 'either an exclusionary rule or an immunity which deprived [the applicants] of access to court'. But that was not quite the end of the story. The

[113] At paras 160–164.
[114] *Z and others v United Kingdom* (2001) 34 EHRR 97.
[115] C. Gearty, 'Osman Unravels' (2002) 65 *MLR* 87.

ECtHR went on to find that ECHR Article 13 had been breached: no effective remedy had been made available for a grave violation of ECHR Article 3.

Now it could be argued that this ruling was of limited scope, since the case antedated the introduction of the Human Rights Act 1998, which may (or may not) be read as providing a new and adequate remedy for violations of human rights. It is nonetheless a severe finding, since alternative avenues of redress did in fact exist and the victims had in fact *already received compensation* under the terms of the Criminal Injuries Compensation Scheme.[116] The ECtHR did not go so far as to say that *only* a judicial remedy was adequate to furnish effective redress but it certainly hinted as much; the judgment points to the advantages of *judicial* proceedings in affording 'strong guarantees of independence, access for the victim and family and enforceability of awards'.[117] Moreover, the ECtHR laid great emphasis on the importance of *monetary compensation* as a remedy for violation of individual rights, at least where the right violated was as fundamental as the right to life or the prohibition against torture, inhuman and degrading treatment here in issue. And the damages awarded under ECHR Article 41, although once again said to be assessed on an equitable basis, were far from negligible: in respect of what was described as 'very serious abuse and neglect over a period of more than four years', the three applicants gained a total of £112,000 for pecuniary damage, with £32,000 per child for non-pecuniary damage—a good deal more, be it said, than the UK government considered appropriate. It was also much more than they had been awarded under the Criminal Injuries Compensation Scheme, set up to cover precisely the situation of these cases, where the state stands surety for the victims of criminal acts for which it is not technically responsible.[118] Again, this is a severe ruling.

---

[116] *Z and others v UK*, above note 112, at paras 105–11.

[117] At para 109.

[118] At para 49 of the *Osman* judgment, it is noted that the Board had awarded £1,000 to Z, £3,000 to A and B, and £2,000 to C in respect of physical and psychological injury suffered at the hands of their parents.

Even when it is admitted that it is exceptional not to award damages in ECHR Article 3 cases, it should be borne in mind that the state is usually the primary actor in such cases.[119] This case involved an omission; the primary wrongdoers were the parents and neither the state nor its officials were guilty of abuse. The state was, in short, being held responsible for a supervisory function and for failure by a public service to react to an allegedly grave and distressing situation. For the state, a huge extension of liability from misfeasance to non-feasance; for the ECtHR, a big leap forward from negative to affirmative remedies. There is, however, no trace in the judgment that the Court understood the enormity of the step it was taking, nor has it ever properly sought to delimit the boundaries of these novel affirmative obligations.

In a sharp change of jurisdictions, the controversial Canadian case of *Doe v Metropolitan Toronto Board of Commissioners of Police*[120] falls to be considered. *Doe* was overtly a test case,[121] set down in the name of a young woman who had been attacked and raped, but effectively fought by women's groups. They sponsored an action in negligence, alleging that the crime had been facilitated, if not caused, by the (wilful) failure of the Toronto police to issue warnings of danger posed to young women by the presence in the city of an undetected serial rapist. A violation of the Canadian Charter of Fundamental Rights and Freedoms was also pleaded, fairly summarized as an allegation of 'institutional sexism' against the police. There had been a period of

See also paras 112–131, where the views of the British government on quantum are set out. For the Criminal Injuries Compensation Scheme, see further Chap. 3 text at note 38.

[119] *Aydin v Turkey* (1998) 25 EHRR 251.

[120] *Doe v Metropolitan Toronto Board of Commissioners of Police* (1989) 58 DLR (4th) 396 affirmed at (1990) 74 OR (2d) 225 (Div Ct). The comparison has already been made by Hoyano, above note 105, whose argument is rather different.

[121] See M. Randall, 'Sex Discrimination, Accountability of Public Authorities and the Public/Private Divide in Tort Law: An Analysis of Doe v Metropolitan Toronto (Municipality) Board of Commissioners of Police' (2001) 26 *Queen's LJ* 45.

collaboration and negotiation between police and women's groups on the appropriate response to rape cases, but these had broken down and, in the twelve years that passed between issue of writ and final decision, the police had apparently refused to engage seriously in negotiations. Thus, in contrast to *Osman* and *Z*, the *Doe* case involved a serious dispute over policy and a political resolution had been attempted but failed. This lends support to the view that *Doe* was a concealed judicial review action or attempt at 'collateral review' that should either have been 'transferred in' to the appropriate jurisdiction or, in the event of success, have culminated in a declaratory judgment.[122] Somewhat surprisingly, however, the trial judge found sufficient proximity between police and claimant for them to owe her a duty of care to warn of the special danger she faced as a member of a vulnerable group. This idiosyncratic finding was backed up by a deterrent award of over $220,000 in damages (with costs of up to $5 million).

The case against warning made by the police is contained in an internal police report released during the proceedings. We have met these arguments before, in the context of deterrent theories of tort law. The report raises the spectre of defensive policing, claiming that a decision in favour of the claimant would cause officers to 'second-guess themselves instead of making the tough investigative decisions that are necessary'. Success would also 'open the door to attacking the police by means of civil lawsuits for damages challenging criminal investigations from years past'. Consequently, the police would be forced to spend time and money defending previous investigations instead of suppressing crime, and would be reluctant to be 'self-critical and provide constructive criticism of their own

---

[122] S. Childs and P. Ceyssens, '*Doe v Metropolitan Toronto Board of Commissioners of Police* and the Status of Public Oversight of the Police in Canada' (1998) 36 *Alberta L Rev.* 1000, citing the contrasting cases of *Clubb v Saanich (District)* (1996) 46 LR 4th 253 (Canada) and *R v Chief Constable* of N Wales ex p AB [1998] 3 WLR 57 (England). See also *Hill v Chief Constable of Yorkshire* [1988] 2 All ER 238.

organization' for fear that it would lead to civil liability.[123] This is a strong and arguably somewhat cynical version of the 'decision trap' or 'competing pressures' argument I advanced in my last lecture. The case advanced by the women's groups was that the police had not engaged and do not normally engage in open and critical self-reflection. The service is introverted and notably impervious to external criticism. In the instant case, representations from the public had been ignored although, in the event, the police had been unable to persuade a senior member of the judiciary of the correctness of their policies.

A 'decision trap' then for the judges. On the one hand stands the classical, Diceyan rule of law argument, based on symbolic deterrence, that no legal system can afford to turn a blind eye to instances of disgraceful conduct, especially on the part of public authorities. The main purpose of the legal system being corrective justice, it must provide redress and, if it falls to tort law to exact accountability, then so be it.[124] The force of this argument is strengthened when a violation of human rights is involved. It is clearly an embarrassment for judges to have to say of a right with constitutional status that it merits a lesser remedy than those available in traditional tort actions.[125] When the right invoked overlaps with

---

[123] A confidential report of the Toronto police authorities, produced during litigation and quoted by Randall, above note 121.

[124] The position finds expression generally in the two monographs of T. R. S. Allan, *Law, Liberty and Justice, The Legal Foundations of British Constitutionalism* (Oxford: Oxford University Press, 1993) and *Constitutional Justice* (Oxford: Oxford University Press, 2001). See also *M v Home Office* [1993] 3 WLR 433 (Lord Woolf).

[125] S. 24 of the Canadian Charter of Rights and Freedoms provides that 'Anyone whose rights and freedoms as guaranteed by this Charter have been infringed or denied may apply to a court of competent jurisdiction to obtain such remedy as the court considers appropriate and just in the circumstances.' It has been held in *R v McGillivray* (1990) 56 CCC (3d) 304, 306 by Rice JA that Charter damages should resemble those usually awarded in tort cases but should not necessarily be restricted thereto. See for further discussion Pilkington, 'Damages as a Remedy for Infringement of the Canadian Charter of Rights and Freedoms' (1984) 62 *Can. Bar Rev.* 517; K. Cooper-Stephenson, 'Tort Theory for the Charter Damages Remedy' (1988) 52 *Saskachewan LR* 1; D. Mullan, 'Damages for Violation of Constitutional Rights—A False Spring? (1996) 6 *NJCL* 105.

or mirrors a standard tort action, the embarrassment will be the greater.[126] Again, human rights documents are typically individual in character. The rights vest in individuals and, as with tort law, create expectations of individuated judgments, and the individuated awards of damages made in such cases give the impression of being affordable when the defendant is the state or a large public authority. It is the knowledge of the class claim lurking in the background that creates the problem.

It is now time to pick up and reconsider in the context of transnational litigation arguments concerning resource allocation touched on in the previous lecture. Setting the case law in context, I shall suggest that the impact is almost certain to create drains on scarce resources and likely also to skew the process of resource allocation, favouring those classes and categories of expenditure which have recently been touched by a successful tort or state liability action.[127] Since both the seminal domestic case of *X (Minors) v Bedford-shire*[128] and the ECtHR decisions in *Osman* and *Z v United Kingdom* concerned children, I shall concentrate on policies concerning children. A further reason to focus on this area is that it is the subject of the new and free-standing Convention on the Rights of the Child, brokered by the United Nations and policed by its Committee on Human Rights. In consequence, the subject is a topical one, high on the political agenda of the Blair government, highly sympathetic to

---

[126] As in *Simpson v AG (Baigent's* case) [1994] 3 NZLR 667, discussed by M. Taggart, 'Tugging on Superman's Cape: Lessons from Experience with the New Zealand Bill of Rights Act 1990' [1998] *PL* 266. The famous US case of *Bivens v Six Unknown Named Agents of Federal Bureau of Narcotics* 403 US 388 (1971) also introduces the concept of 'constitutional wrong' to cover a situation where, due to the barrier against suits in federal courts brought by citizens of one state against another state, a tort action was not available, although the facts of the case amounted to a tort.

[127] On the tendency of administrators to leave out of account distant experience of unfavourable court cases see G. Richardson and M. Sunkin, 'Judicial Review: Questions of Impact' [1996] *PL* 79.

[128] *X (Minors) v Bedfordshire, M v Newham LBC* [1995] 2 AC 633, which concerned the respective liability of education authorities to children with special needs and of local authority social services departments for the exercise of statutory powers under the Children Acts.

the issue, in proof of which it has just announced its intention to create a new post of Children's Commissioner, with a view to strengthening the machinery for protection of children's rights.[129]

A convenient starting point for discussion of the second raft of cases in *X (Minors) v Bedfordshire*, in which the House of Lords laid down the no-liability rule challenged in *Z v United Kingdom*, is the somewhat similar case of *Re S*,[130] referred to the House of Lords several years later, after the introduction of the Human Rights Act. In issue here were failures by local authorities adequately to implement child-care orders, the central question being whether the statutory system, modern and brought into force after consideration by an inter-departmental working party,[131] was compatible with human rights law, in that it did not provide for supervision by a court. In his speech in the House, Lord Nicholls took care to set out the dimensions of the problem. Citing figures provided by the government, he said:[132]

Over the last six years there has been a steady increase in the number of children looked after by local authorities in England and Wales. At present there are 36,400 children accommodated under care orders, compared with 28,500 in 1995, an increase of

[129] See Ninth Report of the Joint Committee on Human Rights, *The Case for a Children's Commissioner for England*, HL 96/HC 666 (2002–03); *The Government's Response to the Case for a Children's Commissioner for England*, HL 187/HC 1279 (2002–03); *The Government's Response to the Committee's Ninth Report on the Case for a Children's Commissioner for England. The Government's Response to the Case for a Children's Commissioner for England*, HL 13/HC 135 (2003–04). And see DFES, Green Paper, *Every Child Matters*, 8 September 2003, www.dfes.gov.uk/everychild

[130] *Re S, Re W (Children) (Care Order. Implementation Care Plan)* [2002] 2 WLR 720, noted by J. Herring, 'The Human Rights of Children in Care' (2002) 118 *LQR* 234. The application was for an order that Parts III and IV of the Children Act 1989 were incompatible with the Human Rights Act 1988.

[131] 'Review of Child Care Law' (September 1985). The operation of the Children Act had been reviewed as recently as 1997 by Sir William Utting and the government response to this review published as Cm 4105 (1998). The steps taken to improve child care law are set out at length in the judgment of Lord Nicholls at paras 27–33.

[132] At para 29.

27 per cent. In addition local authorities provide accommodation for nearly 20,000 children . . . in need. A decade's experience in the operation of the Act, at a time of increasing demands on local authorities, has shown that there are occasions when, with the best will in the world, local authorities' discharge of their parental responsibilities has not been satisfactory. The system does not always work well. Shortages of money, of suitable trained staff and of suitable foster carers and prospective adopters for difficult children are among the reasons. There have been delays in placing children in accordance with their care plans, unsatisfactory breakdown rates and delays in finding substitute placements.

Hidden in this passage is an interesting variant of the traditional floodgates argument, concerning the capacity of courts successfully to carry out supervisory functions. They too may suffer shortages of money and suitably trained staff. We know, for example, from media investigations that the guardian *ad litem* system, operated by the Children and Family Court Advisory Service (CAFCAS), already has to handle more than 30,000 cases annually and is under severe pressure, threatened by a lack of resources and manpower. At the end of 2003, a backlog existed of 500 cases and delays of six weeks in bringing cases to court could be expected in even the most urgent of cases.[133] To give to the courts new supervisory functions, as the House of Lords was asked in *Re S* to do, would clearly create a further pressure on resources, add to the delays, and require further government funding.

And this is not the worst news. In 2002, the UN Committee on the Rights of the Child published a periodic report highly critical of the United Kingdom's record on children's rights.[134] It singled out for particular mention 'the high proportion of children living in poverty'; the lack of an 'effective co-ordinated poverty eradication strategy'; youth homelessness; the poor quality of accommodation for

---

[133] *Observer*, 21 September 2003. Some weeks before, a BBC Analysis report had tackled the subject in greater detail: *Court Delays Endanger Vulnerable Children*, 8 July 2003.
[134] CRC/C/15/Add 188.

asylum-seekers; and the large numbers of children incarcerated in prisons. We know too that around four million children live in poverty, one million of them in dire poverty. Three thousand young people are in custody, of whom around 80 per cent are re-convicted within two years.[135] The UN Committee noted also that the Convention had not been incorporated into domestic law and, expressing concern at the absence of central government co-ordinating machinery, recommended an analysis of all sectoral and total budgets, devolved or otherwise, with a view to identifying priorities and allocating resources effectively to the maximum extent possible.[136] This goes rather further than even a series of tort judgments can go. Yet one year later, the Children's Rights Alliance, reviewing progress, found little evidence of improvement. These shocking statistics set the context against which *Z v United Kingdom* was decided and in which the deterrent effects of tort law fall to be evaluated.

The background against which claims of children with special educational needs (SEN) to compensation covering a placement in a private school or, long after the event, recognition of the loss of a chance to have had special educational needs acknowledged and catered for, is somewhat similar. The overall sums available are, on the face of things, large. The Blair government prioritizes education and, following a White Paper,[137] pledged £37 million in targeted support for SEN. Parents of SEN children naturally tend to see this budget as earmarked for SEN children, and do not always appreciate that it can be used for general upgrading of the schools to which SEN children are increasingly allocated and for which they may often create special problems. The sum available to a small education authority or individual school is very much smaller and the SEN budget could easily be exhausted by an award of damages to cover private school fees, bearing in mind that these

---

[135] Statistics collected by the Children's Rights Alliance and cited in the *Guardian*, 9 October 2003.

[136] CRC/C/15/Add. 188, Recommendation 11.

[137] *Excellence for all Children: Meeting Special Educational Needs* (Cmnd 3785 (1998)

range from £5,000 to £50,000 annually. Perhaps this is why the most recent legislation precludes the tribunals hearing claims relating to discrimination and temporary exclusions from awarding compensation.[138]

What sort of message do these cases convey? That social workers should move quickly to take 'at risk' children into care? But isn't that to make wholly unwarranted assumptions about the quality of care in children's homes? Sixty thousand children are currently in local authority care, 90 per cent of whom have been abused or suffer parental neglect, a figure that has risen by 22 per cent since 1994. To be taken into care seriously affects someone's life chances: about 50 per cent of children in care leave school with no qualifications and just 4 per cent get five GCSEs. There are darker stories too. The Irish government currently faces claims, following an offer of compensation to victims of child abuse in institutions oper-ated by the Catholic Church, some of which go back as far as the 1920s. The sums involved are said to total more than £725 million and a special tribunal, presided over by a judge, established to handle the multiplicity of claims, has been swamped.[139] Sadly, this is just one of a series of global scan-dals concerning treatment in children's homes.[140] And aren't social workers who move too quickly at risk of litigation by parents for violation of their ECHR Article 8 rights? That is surely the message of the *East Berkshire* cases,[141] a message with added resonance in the light of reports that several thousand cases decided by the Family Courts, in

---

[138] The Special Educational Needs and Disability Act 2001. Arguably, the exclusion is dysfunctional, as tending to push claims for compen-sation into the courts.

[139] *Daily Telegraph*, 2 October 2003.

[140] See the English cases of *Trotman v N. Yorkhire CC* [1999] LGR 584; *Lister v Hesely AHA* [2001] 2 WLR 1311. A worker in a care home has recently had his conviction for child abuse quashed, raising allegations that this and similar convictions were secured by improper promises to potential witnesses that they could receive compensation if they made complaints. A class action is being considered by the Historical Abuse Appeal Panel, a grouping of solicitors handling such cases: *The Times*, 6 January 2004.

[141] *JD and others v East Berkshire Community Health Trust and others* [2003] EWCA Civ 1151, discussed more fully in Chap. 1 at note 75.

which children have been taken from their parents on the advice of expert medical evidence now considered flawed, may have to be re-opened. Which of these messages ring the loudest bells? What sort of compensation should be made? What is the best way to use the limited resources? The sums involved are enormous and the claims on government funding almost infinite. Theoretically, the problem can be pushed back by courts to government and Parliament to 'put a penny on the income tax'. But they too now face a restricted field of manoeuvre.

CONCLUSIONS

Transnational courts are growing up and seeking to re-inforce their standing and carve out a significant role for law in the new world order. They wish to play a central part in debates over internationalism, global transformation, and the reach of transnational courts. They want to redefine the new world order as a legal hierarchy, in which their cosmopolitan legal norms are accorded overarching, universal status. They want to see their law enforced. Their toolkits seem deficient without mandatory remedies and, more useful because less intrusive, the power of sanction contained in a finding of liability and award of damages. Consequently, as I have tried to show in this lecture, they have been moving rapidly from 'defensive' or 'negative' to 'affirmative' remedies. Instead of contenting themselves with standard-setting, issuing declaratory judgments that establish the parameters within which the state must act, transnational courts have begun to make forays on to areas of national sovereignty and incursions deep into the territory of distributive justice. As increasingly courts dictate positive intervention by society, 'aggregative' and 'distributive' political 'principles'[142] are becoming confused. In consequence, the share of collective goods assigned by courts to individuals for their personal use is beginning to impinge

---

[142] See Introduction at note 8.

on the share at the disposal of government and public
authorities for the collective benefit of the community.

Judicial attitudes to remedies are also changing, as courts
scramble to complete their toolkits with a set of power tools.
Injunctive relief, the most potent and intrusive remedy,[143] is
perilous for transnational courts, whose orders have to be
addressed directly to sovereign states. This hard political
truth is recognized by the machinery of the Committee of
Ministers, designed to ensure that ECtHR rulings are treated
with respect and carried into effect. Damages are less
threatening and intrusive than mandatory orders, although
they can still be seen to serve purposes of sanction and
accountability. The cases we are now seeing take intrusion
rather further by using the new affirmative remedies to
reinforce the concept of affirmative rights (defined earlier
to mean rights which impose affirmative duties on governments to intervene to redress deprivations in society). Thus
the admonition that everyone's life shall be protected by
law, which enjoins the state to refrain from taking life 'intentionally', is transmuted into an obligation 'to take appropriate steps to guard life'.[144] When we know that this
citation comes from a Commission case involving adverse
reaction to vaccination, we can see how deeply courts may
penetrate the territory of governmental policy-making
under the banner of affirmative economic and social rights.
The instrument of state liability can also be deployed to
impose affirmative duties on individuals—a route, I have
suggested, not without its perils!

Against the argument, in my view fallacious, that an
order for financial reparation forces states squarely to face
up to collective injustice we must set the realist view that

---

[143] P. Schuck, *Suing Government: Citizen Remedies for Official Wrongs*
(New Haven, Conn.: Yale University Press, 1983) at 150 calls the injunc-
tion 'a powerful instrument of specific deterrence', capable of achieving
'a more specific, predictable and rapid change in official behaviour than
damage remedies can accomplish'.

[144] *X v United Kingdom*, Application no 7154/75, 14 DR 31 (1978). The
Commission found the state system of control and supervision to be
sufficient: see D. O'Sullivan, 'The Allocation of Scarce Resources and
the Right to Life under the ECHR' [1998] *PL* 389.

non-compliance seldom amounts to deliberate wrong-doing. Typically, non-compliance with human rights standards or court orders is, like bureaucratic negligence, deviant behaviour that is as unintended as it is endemic. It is more likely to respond to political measures of assistance and persuasion than to the coercive sanctions, fines, and awards of damages that drain the resources of public services.[145] Compensation regimes, as Tomuschat argues, are only really workable and effective 'during fair weather periods in countries which, by and large, respect the rule of law'. Even then, there is grave risk of 'whiplash'. For this amongst other reasons, Tomuschat regards a uniform system of reparation for individuals as unworkable and favours the traditional pattern of collective settlement.[146] Salutary warnings, suggesting a little more modesty and forbearance on the part of transnational jurisdictions: carrot rather than stick!

---

[145] A. Chayes and A. Chayes, 'On Compliance' (1993) 47 *International Organizations* 175.

[146] Tomuschat, above note 46, at 20–1.

# 3

# Administrative Compensation: Brave New World?

As suggested in the previous lecture, when used by lawyers the term 'compensation' is troublesome. In much the same way as the ambiguous notion of distributive justice, it is capable of leaping the boundary between law and politics; alternatively, it may be used precisely to denote that boundary. The term *ex gratia* compensation, for example, is frequently used to suggest that an award is not justiciable. Single *ex gratia* payments are commonly used to rectify minor administrative failings or mark an abnormal loss suffered by a citizen.[1] A 'one off' award of compensation may also follow from an ombudsman recommendation or represent a negotiated settlement of litigation.

Administrative compensation, however, covers a much wider field, and much of it is statutory in origin. Although tort lawyers tend to think first of accident compensation, the subject-matter of statutory compensation plans is actually very varied. Compensation in case of requisition of property for public purposes is, for example, extensive and widely recognized. In the depths of history, its origins may be traced back to Crown practices of *ex gratia* compensation but they are usually said to lie in the practice of the legislature in seventeenth-century Britain and the 'no taking' principle protected in the American Constitution.[2]

---

[1] The basis of *ex gratia* payment is explained in C. Harlow, *Compensation and Government Torts* (London: Sweet and Maxwell, 1982) at 117–21. And see *Maladministration and Redress*, HC 112 (1994/5) below.

[2] J. W. Ely Jr, 'That Due Satisfaction may be Made: the Fifth Amendment and the Origins of the Compensation Principle' 36 *Am. J of Legal History* 1 (1992); F. Michelman, 'Property, Utility and Fairness:

In modern times, the collective responsibility to compensate for activities carried on in the public interest is widely recognized in planning legislation, which puts in place statutory schemes in respect of expropriation of private property and sometimes extends more widely to loss in the form of 'planning blight'.[3] These schemes are in fact very expensive and the sums involved may be sufficiently crippling to act as a deterrent to development. Similarly, pay-outs to farmers after the BSE crisis (or in the Milk Quotas saga discussed in my previous lecture) ran into many millions, even though widely contested by the farming community as inadequate.

Short-term compensation schemes may be put in place to deal with a crisis situation or to resolve a specific problem, such as an unexpected epidemic of animal disease in a case not already covered by legislation. A supplementary compensation plan had, for example, to be put in place for farmers affected by the salmonella epidemic in eggs and poultry, a situation covered in principle by existing statute, following the revelation in the course of an ombudsman investigation that the terms of the statutory plan had been deliberately misapplied by the ministry.[4] These schemes may or may not be statutory in character, though the scale of the payments usually points towards statutory authorization. (The British Criminal Injuries Compensation Scheme was exceptional in being initiated as an *ex gratia* scheme, but the scale of the payments was a factor in the consistent pressure to put the scheme on to a statutory basis.) The state has often assumed responsibility for loss

Comments on the Ethical Foundations of "Just Compensation" Law' 80 *Harv. L Rev.* 1165 (1967).

[3] See, e.g., the Land Compensation Act 1973. And see the dispute over the proper ambit of planning blight relief in 'The Channel Tunnel Link and Blight: Investigation of Complaints against the Department of Transport', HC 193 (1994/5).

[4] *Compensation to Farmers for Slaughtered Poultry*, HC 519 (1992/3), cited in C. Harlow and R. W. Rawlings, *Law and Administration* (2nd edn, London: Butterworths, 1997) at 608. The affair might now form the basis of an action for misfeasance in public office: see text below at note 21.

caused through the failure of private sector bodies, such as banks, brokers, or insurers, more especially when the state has assumed or is deemed by public opinion to have regulatory functions. This is a significant dimension of the risk-averse society towards which, I suggested in the Introduction to these lectures, we are fast progressing.[5] This type of compensation stokes the fires of the 'compensation culture', as victims whose cases lie on the border-line or involve similar situations protest that they have been unfairly excluded. Compensation may relate very closely to legal liability, bringing pressure on courts to extend the boundaries of law. A compensation scheme may represent a settlement of legal liability or be set up in response to the initiation of a class action, a slightly different situation. Class actions may represent a step in the political battle for compensation, bringing settlements bargained in the shadow of the law. Without admitting responsibility, government is often prepared to compensate, sometimes after a recommendation from an ombudsman. The compensation culture is in this way heightened, as the two systems are played off against each other. (An alternative way to describe this phenomenon might be as a variation of the 'cascade effect' described in my second lecture.)

Without attempting any more precise definition of compensation, it is helpful to distinguish the different types. I have suggested a division according to the three rather different situations with which compensation deals:

  (i) large-scale, statutory, and ongoing compensation schemes, such as land compensation or accident compensation plans;
 (ii) small-scale statutory compensation, to deal with situations thought to be temporary;
(iii) individuated *ex gratia* payments.

Cane and Atiyah, however, look at compensation from a slightly different angle, as embracing three separate types

---

[5] C. Fisher, 'The Rise of the Risk Commonwealth and the Challenge for Administrative Law' [2003] *PL* 455.

of redress.[6] They also identify three different types of compensation but focus on the type of injury. Thus compensation may be awarded:

    (i) as an equivalent for what has been lost, as is the case with legal damages;

    (ii) as a substitute or solace for what has been lost, as with the bereavement payment awarded for the loss of a child;

    (iii) in respect of what the victim has never had in comparison with others in a similar situation.

Clearly, there may be overlap between the first two categories, while the third moves well on to the territory of distributive justice. This categorization reflects the subtle distinction between liability and remedies pursued in the previous lecture. It is also relevant to many of the human rights cases discussed there.

This lecture seeks to explore, without necessarily disentangling, the tangled relationships between liability, damages, and compensation. I shall argue that the failure to distinguish clearly between compensation in the context of legal liability and responsibility in the wider context of distributive justice has done much to fuel the litigation fever that is a mark of contemporary society. I shall argue that the 'compensation culture' is not confined within legal boundaries. The relationship is a complex and subtle one. Compensation reinforces pressure for an expansive tort law; expanding tort law augments the flood of litigation; both feed back into the political process, accentuating pressure for state compensation.

## ACCIDENT COMPENSATION

The most complete transfer of private to public law is the accident compensation plan—a point not overlooked by

---

[6] P. Cane, *Atiyah's Accidents, Compensation and the Law* (hereafter Cane and Atiyah) (6th edn, London: Butterworths, 1999) at 402.

personal injuries lawyers! Yet public lawyers, for whom the focal point of the administrative law world has been the steady rise and consolidation of the judicial review action, have tended to overlook the significance of the transfer. While much ink has been spent on the artificial boundary disputes and conceptual dissonances that have developed,[7] the terrain of administrative compensation has largely been ceded to private lawyers.

This is not the place for an audit of accident compensation schemes, nor am I the right person to conduct one; the task is primarily one for economists and statisticians. In any event, the seminal work, which has very much influenced my thinking, has already been written.[8] All that I can hope to do here is to look briefly at the arguments surrounding accident compensation in much the same way as, in the two previous lectures, I looked at tort law and state liability. It is reasonable, for example, closely to scrutinize the argument that accident compensation is intrinsically fairer and more equal than tort law since, if that argument is undercut, there is less reason to replace the tort system. After all, ordinary people understand tort law. It seems to them to place the responsibility for compensation on those deemed to be wrongdoers and to be based on a set 'of familiar and intuitively compelling ideas about responsibility and justice'.[9] Similarly, the argument that accident compensation penalizes the most seriously injured is considerable. A compensation plan in the hands of government is an easy target for retrenchment, carrying the constant threat that benefits will be down-rated and reduced to the 'safety net' level of other vital welfare services. Advocates of state compensation have to appeal to

---

[7] A debate updated and usefully encapsulated by P. Cane, 'Accountability and the Public/Private Distinction' in P. Leyland and N. Bamforth (eds), *Public Law in a Multi-Layered Constitution* (Oxford: Hart Publishing, 2003).

[8] P. S. Atiyah, *Accidents, Compensation and the Law* (London: Weidenfeld and Nicolson, 1970), now Cane and Atiyah, above note 6.

[9] A. Ripstein, 'Some Recent Obituaries of Tort Law' (1998) 48 *UTLJ* 561, 574.

social solidarity, a sentiment to which the taxpayer may not always subscribe. It can then be argued that it is a major injustice to deprive the seriously injured of their right to chance their luck in and claim the greater prizes offered by the 'forensic lottery',[10] an opportunity that we have seen aggrandized as the fundamental 'right to a court'. This reasoning is unfair. Retrenchment is no more an argument against administrative compensation than the present soaring rates of damages are an argument for tort law. The case for administrative compensation is that advanced by Cohen: that it permits proper management of public resources.[11] This must carry the implication that, if public retrenchment is considered necessary, there is no particular reason why the losses should fall on pensioners or the recipients of welfare benefits rather than on accident victims. Of course, good reasons can be advanced but society is entitled to evaluate them.

Sadly, there are few in-depth empirical studies of administrative compensation schemes.[12] We have nonetheless accumulated enough experience to know that administrative compensation is not a panacea. In the United Kingdom, the 'sad and sorry' history of vaccine damage compensation has taught us that the best intentions of politicians and legislators can be foiled by reluctance and parsimony on

---

[10] The lottery metaphor was famously introduced by T. Ison, *The Forensic Lottery* (London: Staples Press, 1967). D. Harris *et al.*, *Compensation and Support for Illness and Injury* (Oxford: Clarendon, 1984) use the metaphor of an obstacle race. In defence of the right to sue see R. Mahoney, 'New Zealand's Accident Compensation Scheme: A Reassessment', 40 AJCL 159, 162 (1992) and L. Klar, 'New Zealand's Accident Compensation Scheme: A Tort Lawyer's Perspective' in F. Steel and S. Rodgers-Magnet (eds), *Issues in Tort Law* (Toronto: Carswell, 1983).

[11] D. Cohen, 'Tort Law and the Crown: Administrative Compensation and the Modern State' in K. Cooper-Stephenson and E. Gibson (eds), *Tort Theory* (York: Captus University Publications, 1993) at 361.

[12] There is a vast American empirical literature on automobile plans and, as already stated, D. Dewes, D. Duff, and M. Trebilcock, *Exploring the Domain of Accident Law, Taking the Facts Seriously* (New York: Oxford University Press, 1996) test evidence on the efficacy of compensation plans in the field of traffic, medical mishap, products, environmental and workplace liability.

the part of administrators.[13] Delay has emerged as a
feature of compensation schemes, just as it is with litigation,
though the delays are normally somewhat less. And,
although sums paid out in accident compensation mount
steadily, the take-up rate is not always higher than in
the tort system.[14] Moreover, compensation plans do not
entirely preclude litigation, though this will normally
take the 'lighter' form of judicial review or resolution by
an administrative tribunal.[15] Around the edges of accident
compensation schemes, however, tort litigation may
be prompted, in an effort to access tort law's higher
damages.

Interest in accident compensation gained force in this
country in the aftermath of the thalidomide tragedy, once
it was appreciated by the public that the common law might
not allow recovery of damages by children who had
suffered birth defects while in the womb, thus leaving
severely disabled infants without adequate financial support.[16] Perhaps surprisingly, no state compensation plan
followed, nor did the Pearson Commission, set up to make
recommendations on law reform in the light of the thalidomide experience, recommend a state-financed accident
compensation scheme. Instead it opted for a 'mixed' system

---

[13] G. Dworkin, 'Compensation and Payments for Vaccine Damage'
[1979] *JSWL* 330; C. Harlow and R. W. Rawlings, *Law and Administration*
(London: Weidenfeld and Nicolson, 1984) at 398–406.

[14] A point tested by P. Davis *et al.*, 'Compensation for Medical Injury
in New Zealand: Does "No-Fault" Increase the Level of Claims Making
and Reduce Social and Clinical Selectivity?' (2002) 27 *J of Health Politics,
Policy and Law* 833.

[15] *R v Criminal Injuries Compensation Board ex p Lain* [1967] 2 QB 864
established the justiciability of the Criminal Injuries Compensation
Scheme, initially an *ex gratia* scheme, which made no provision for
review or appeal. Since then the parameters and interpretation of the
Scheme have been tested by judicial review many times: ten cases in the
years 1991–9 are recorded. The majority of schemes do, however, allow
for appeal to an administrative tribunal, if not always the courts. Complaint may also be made to an ombudsman.

[16] This was because (perhaps arguably) the common law did not
recognize the right of an unborn child to bring an action. The point was
settled by the Congenital Disabilities (Civil Liability) Act 1976.

of fault, no-fault and strict liability,[17] an outcome widely seen as a missed opportunity[18] (though not perhaps by practitioners). Perhaps the Commission sensed a change in the political climate—it reported after all only one year before Margaret Thatcher was first elected—perhaps it was bought off by lawyers or, like the trade unions that gave evidence to Pearson, persuaded by the 'golden handshake' argument for the forensic lottery.

It was left to Atiyah, in his study of accident compensation, first published in 1970,[19] to underline the nature of the problem: the inadequacy of the social security system. Atiyah also highlighted a number of problems with compensation plans. He took issue with the manifest inequalities they introduced: need was never the sole criterion; the system treated disease differently from disability, disability differently from industrial illness and both differently from illness and so on. Further inequity was caused when partial compensation plans, aimed at specific forms of injury, such as vaccine damage or criminal violence, were introduced to run alongside inadequate social security benefits. But partial or 'mixed' schemes, in which no-fault compensation ran alongside tort liability, allowing victims a choice, were not cost effective. Atiyah was nonetheless driven to the conclusion that:[20]

since such a relatively small number of injured people receive compensation under the tort system, and given that the administrative cost is so substantial, it is necessary to ask very seriously whether the tort system is worth what it costs. It is difficult to answer that question other than negatively.

New Zealand was the first common law country wholeheartedly to embrace accident compensation. The Woodhouse Report once again condemned the tort system as a 'virtual lottery', worsened by the costs of administering the

---

[17] Report of the Royal Commission on Civil Liability for Personal Injuries, Cmnd 7054 (1978).

[18] E.g., D. Allen, C. Bourne, and J. Holyoak (eds), *Accident Compensation after Pearson* (London: Sweet and Maxwell, 1979).

[19] Cane and Atiyah, above note 6.

[20] Ibid., at 415.

system, which absorbed 50 per cent of expenditure.[21] The no-fault accident compensation plan (ACS) recommended by Woodhouse was introduced in 1974, at a high point of belief in 'cradle-to-grave' social welfare[22] and was implemented on an incremental basis by a series of statutes.[23] Over the years, the ACS has, in common with many welfare schemes, been subject to some retrenchment and has not altogether escaped the itch to privatize, at least temporarily,[24] but the socialistic flavour is retained in the most recent legislation, which describes the overriding purpose as being 'to enhance the public good and reinforce the social contract represented by the first accident compensation scheme'. Briefly, the ACS, which now covers compensation for accident, medical misadventure, occupational disease, and criminal injuries, is administered by the Accident Compensation Corporation (ACC) and up to a point financed by contributions from employers, employees, car owners, and the medical profession.

This system of mixed finance helps to meet the perennial objections that state compensation takes business from or, more usually, represents an unwarranted subsidy to the private insurance industry. The general taxation fund need not necessarily bear the total cost of compensation plans with the private sector escaping scot-free. Motoring

[21] *Report of the Royal Commission of Inquiry into Compensation for Personal Injury in New Zealand* (The Woodhouse Report) (1967) at 3, noted by Mathieson (1968) 31 *MLR* 544.

[22] B. Lichtenstein, 'From Principle to Parsimony: A Critical Analysis of New Zealand's No-Fault Accident Compensation Scheme' (1999) 12 *Social Justice Research* 99, 100 describes the ACC as a completion of the 'cultural expectations of the benefits promised in the 1930s by the Labour Party'.

[23] The Accident Compensation Act 1972 was modified, then replaced by the Accident Rehabilitation and Compensation Insurance Act 1992, which instituted a 'user pays' scheme, and reformed again by the Accident Insurance Act 1998. The Accident Insurance Amendment and Accident Insurance (Transitional Provisions) Act 2000 eliminated the possibility of private workplace insurance.

[24] An initial plan for insurers to run the scheme was rejected after their tenders proved uncompetitive: D. Harris, 'Accident Compensation in New Zealand: A Comprehensive Insurance System' (1974) 37 *MLR* 361 at note 17. In 1998, a private insurance element was introduced but quickly eliminated. For the history of retrenchment see T. Ison, 'Changes to the Accident Compensation System: An International Perspective' (1993) 23 *VUWLR* 25.

is, for example, an activity that should be asked to bear its own costs—an idea that may need also to be asked of railways. It goes without saying that employers should bear their share of the growing cost of accidents at work, if only to ward off arguments about deterrence. There are, too, feasible alternatives to privatization that ought at least to be given serious consideration, such as contribution by insurers or funding through hypothecated taxes, an innovation unpopular with the exchequer but increasingly on the agenda of political parties. In the case of medical accident, patient contributions may even be feasible. Compensation plans do not, after all, differ greatly in this respect from social security or pensions, the funding of which is currently the cause of much political concern.[25] On the other hand, it was the perception, accurate or not, that employers were disproportionately burdened with the costs of accident compensation that, in the 1990s, fuelled the clamour in New Zealand for retrenchment.[26]

A more serious criticism of the ACS is that it makes unfortunate and unfair distinctions between disease, disability, and accidental injury. Like the majority of accident plans it also creates inequity between beneficiaries of the scheme, entitled to income-linked payments, and other less fortunate social security claimants.[27] That this is so undercuts the argument for accident compensation as a clean break with the unfairness of tort law, since accident compensation cannot after all be said to eliminate unfairness. Moreover, the distinctions are inevitably contested, causing the reintroduction of litigation; in this respect the ACC does not differ from other compensation plans in generating 'an expensive body of case law' to test the boundaries of entitlement.[28] This too lends support to the argument for tort law.

---

[25] Alternatives to the welfare state and to privatization are discussed by N. Barr, *The Welfare State as Piggy Bank: Information, Risk, Uncertainty, and the Role of the State* (Oxford: Oxford University Press, 2001).

[26] Lichtenstein, above note 22, at 104.

[27] Cane and Atiyah, above note 6, at 403. See also J. Stapleton, *Disease and the Compensation Debate* (Oxford: Oxford University Press, 1986).

[28] Ison, above note 24, at 37 and similarly, the English CICS, above note 15.

Courts can of course attempt to alleviate the expense of full trial procedure by recourse to modified procedures (such as striking out procedure, that favourite of the Court of Human Rights).

While tort law tends to offer golden handshakes to the most seriously injured, accident compensation is known to advantage the less seriously hurt, a discovery evidenced by the exponential growth in claims to accident compensation schemes. In New Zealand, claims increased from 105,000 in 1975 to almost 1,500,000 claims in 1996–7, with an eighteen-fold increase in benefits. This inevitably raised another perennial accusation, that of fraudulent claims.[29] Caps and thresholds designed to eliminate trivial claims are, however, a prime target for the pro-tort lobby, which invariably depicts them as a deprivation of legal right.[30]

Klar, a strong opponent of the abolition of tort law, takes the view that abolition cannot be without appreciable harm to society. He identifies six benefits other than compensation as flowing from the tort action:[31] that the wrongdoer shall pay; deterrence; appeasement, making it less likely that the victim will retaliate; individuation, in the sense of a remedy tailored to individual needs; education of the public as to what are reasonable and unreasonable standards of conduct; the ombudsman or accountability factor. The theme of these lectures has of course been that many of these benefits are illusory. We should not, however, underplay the extent to which the ideas are 'intuitively compelling', a factor rendering the myths of tort law singularly hard to dislodge.

In fact, rehabilitation has been embedded from the outset as an objective of the ACS, with Woodhouse stressing the vested interest of the community in 'urging forward the physical and economic rehabilitation of every adult

---

[29] Lichtenstein, above note 22, at 104.

[30] Mahoney, above note 10, at 162–3, uses both arguments to argue for reinstatement of tort.

[31] L. Klar, 'New Zealand's Accident Compensation Scheme: A Tort Lawyer's Perspective' in Steel and Rodgers-Magnet, above note 10, at 42.

citizen'.[32] It was nonetheless alleged that workplace accidents increased after the introduction of the ACS, an increase attributed to the absence of fault-based tort liability. This brought into question the effectiveness of the alternative regulatory safety structure, reinforced by heavy criminal penalties but—again allegedly—viewed by courts as well as employers as 'more emphatic than substantive, more educative than coercive, more directory than remedial'.[33] The current legislation is designed both to reinforce rehabilitation and to enhance the preventive duties of the ACC, today reinstated as its primary task. It must too be said that the suggestion of a deterrent effect cuts clean across the experience of tort law,[34] as also the standard literature of regulation,[35] and is quite hard to credit. It is certainly hotly contested by Sir Geoffrey Palmer, a leading proponent of the ACS and largely responsible for it. Palmer denies both potential impact on the incidence of accidents from market-driven safety incentives and also that the scheme has caused 'significant problems of moral hazard to develop'.[36] Whether it is possible for the same institution to combine the function of accident compensation with the

---

[32] Woodhouse Report, above note 21, at 20.

[33] A. Lewis, 'No-fault Liability—Twenty Years' Experience in New Zealand' (1996) 15 *Medicine and Law* 425, 427.

[34] Thus Dewes, Duff, and Trebilcock, above note 12, conclude (Preface, p. v) 'that the deterrent properties of the tort system seem strongest for auto accidents and weakest for environmentally related accidents. The incentive effects of the system are mixed in the case of medical and product-related accidents, making net welfare judgments problematic; in the case of workplace accidents, workers' compensation levies appear to have stronger deterrent effects than the tort system did have or might have if it were resurrected in this context.'

[35] *Inter alia*, R. Baldwin, *Rules and Government* (Oxford: Clarendon, 1995); I. Ayres and J. Braithwaite, *Responsive Regulation: Transcending the Regulation Debate* (Oxford: Oxford University Press, 1992); R. Baldwin and M. Cave, *Understanding Regulation, Theory, Strategy and Practice* (Oxford: Oxford University Press, 1999).

[36] G. Palmer, 'New Zealand's Accident Compensation Scheme' (1994) *UTLJ* 223, 254. The author is a previous Labour Prime Minister and long-time advocate of accident compensation: see G. Palmer, *Compensation for Incapacity: A Study of Law and Social Change in New Zealand and Australia* (Wellington: Oxford University Press, 1979).

regulatory function of accident compensation is a different and perhaps more contestable issue.[37]

Administrative compensation is often said to rest on shaky theoretical foundations, relatively unimportant in the case of a large-scale accident compensation scheme such as the ACS, a scheme of such magnitude that it could scarcely be implemented without resort to legislation, which provides some guarantee of publication and proper debate. Given the contribution made to the economy by the working population, social utility and solidarity are sufficient to underpin a plan which absorbs workers' compensation. Similarly, administrative efficiency would be widely accepted to justify no-fault compensation for medical mishap: a compensation plan takes pressure off an overloaded public health service and relieves health workers. In other cases, state compensation is less easily justified and may be perceived as 'free insurance': the ACS has been regularly targeted for shielding negligent employers and careless drivers; criminal injuries compensation has also been attacked as a 'free insurance scheme for criminals'.[38]

When the idea of 'doing something for victims of criminal violence' was first under consideration in Britain, much time was spent in agonizing over theoretical justification for assuming this new state responsibility. To acknowledge a *legal* duty, based on a failure of security, was unthinkable. The Bishop of Chester spoke grandly in the House of Lords of 'neighbourliness [which] imposes an obligation upon each other to care for the welfare of each other'[39]—an observation that would, no doubt, have given great pleasure to Lord Atkin. A Home Office working party feebly concluded that no constitutional or social principle justifying state compensation could be found; it was, however, happy

---

[37] A. Clayton, 'Some Reflections on Woodhouse and the ACC Legacy' (2003) 34 *VUWLR* 449.

[38] P. Duff, 'The Measure of Criminal Injuries Compensation: Political Pragmatism or Dog's Dinner?' (1998) 8 *OJLS* 105, 106. And see A. Ashworth, 'Punishment and Compensation: Victims, Offenders and the State' (1986) 6 *OJLS* 86.

[39] HL Debs vol 245, col 268.

to proceed on a pragmatic basis. 'The state', it said, 'does nothing for victims of crimes of violence "as such". There is an argument for filling this gap, based mainly on considerations of sympathy for the innocent victim, but falling short of any bounden duty to mitigate the victim's hardship'.[40] Today we should undoubtedly find theoretical support for criminal injuries compensation in the notion of security. But what reason is there really, other than the power and vehemence of the victims' lobby, to single out victims of criminal violence for state compensation, when traffic accident victims were carefully excluded and left to rely on insurance?

Much of the debate surrounding accident compensation in New Zealand is replicated in the debate over criminal injuries compensation in Britain. Not unnaturally, the *ex gratia* foundation of the CICS has always been the focus of complaint from lawyers, though in practice many concessions were made to bring them on board: for example, payments for criminal injuries replicated damages and lawyers staffed the Board that made awards. The move from a scheme mirroring personal injuries damages to the banded tariff scheme introduced in 1995 was a particular target, and was widely, though unfairly, portrayed by lawyers as a disenfranchisement of victims. The CICS has been the object of very wide take-up, with a consistent escalation in claims and in the vast sums paid out in compensation, pegged in principle to damages in tort law. Costs leapt from £33,430 in 1964, the first year of operation, to £109 million in 1992–3, when the (Conservative) government moved to a 'banded tariff' scheme, introduced by the Criminal Injuries Compensation Act 1995. The revised scheme capped claims at a maximum of £500,000 for all but a minority of severely injured victims and imposed a minimum threshold, with a view to excluding trivial claims. Even such relative generosity has never been enough to satisfy the victims' lobby,[41] nor has litigation to test differentials

---

[40] *Compensation for Victims of Violence*, Cmnd 1406 (1961) paras 17–18.
[41] Thus the Victims of Crime Trust is currently using the tragic case of murdered Holly Wells and Jessica Chapman as an argument for uprating

entirely been avoided.[42] The debate is frustratingly inconclusive and preferences for or against the tort system are
largely a matter of belief—or of vested interest, which
should never be underestimated.

Today, a New Zealand-style accident compensation
scheme, whatever its advantages in terms of equity or efficiency, is quite simply not a political runner. The call for
sectional schemes is, however, mounting, more especially
in the field of medical mishap. In Britain, the current initiative for change started with the National Audit Office and
Public Accounts Committee, concerned at the cost of clinical negligence claims to the NHS.[43] A 'Value-for-Money'
audit was undertaken of the procedures, revealing that
there had been a seven-fold rise in reported claims over a
period of seven years.[44] By March 2000, the cost of outstanding claims was assessed at around £2.6 billion with a
further £1.3 billion probably needed to settle unreported
claims—a sum that by no means represented the total
number of outstanding clinical negligence claims, since
claims against GPs and claims originating in the private
sector are both excluded from the statistics. The NAO
report revealed also that the average time between claim
and settlement was five and a half years, a figure that *does
not include litigation;* that a mere 24 per cent of claims funded
by the Legal Services Commission were successful; and
that, in 65 per cent of settlements below £50,000 the legal
and other costs of settling claims exceeded damages

the bereavement payment of £11,000, which they call 'a pittance' and
compare unfavourably (and inaccurately) with civil legal aid: *The Times*,
2 February 2004.

[42] As in *W and D v Meah* [1986] 1 All ER 935, where damages of £6,750
for sexual assault and £10,250 for rape contrasted very favourably with
the awards of £3,000 offered by the CICS.

[43] National Audit Office, 'Handling Clinical Negligence Claims in
England' HC 403 (2000/1). See also Lord Woolf, *Access to Justice, Report
to the Lord Chancellor on the Civil Justice System in England and Wales*
(London: Lord Chancellor's Department, 1996).

[44] In 1999–2000, the NHS received some 10,000 new claims and cleared
9,600, leaving around 23,000 claims outstanding at 31 March 2000: NAO
report, above note 43, executive summary.

awarded. It seems unlikely that, in this area, an administrative compensation scheme could perform less well.

The reaction of the Department of Health to these findings was to publish a consultation paper on options for reform.[45] These are currently under review by a departmental committee set up to examine clinical negligence claims and the way they are handled. This committee has a relatively wide remit: on the one hand, it seeks, by improving the NHS machinery for complaints-handling, to decouple complaints from compensation, in the belief that many complainants are more concerned with explanation and apology than compensation. On the other hand, it is empowered by government to explore the option of no-fault compensation, together with the potential for 'schemes with fixed tariffs for specific injuries'.[46] It is said to be looking at models that could serve as a precedent and also considering the general implications for personal injuries litigation.

A more recent NAO report has looked at compensation in the Ministry of Defence.[47] This revealed that £100 million was paid out in the year 2002–3 to servicemen and women injured through negligence. This represented a four-fold increase over ten years. Further claims of 'hundreds of millions of pounds', which include the disputed Gulf War Veterans' claim, the subject of a major class action, were in the pipeline. To these can now be added claims by serving soldiers, in respect of the inadequacy of the equipment with which they were issued during the war in Iraq. A trickle of claims from Iraqi civilians, said to be the first of their kind, is also reported. The NAO report boldly suggests a direct link between case law, settlement, and compensation, with the huge increase blamed on a sudden rise in levels of personal injuries damages, recently engineered by the

---

[45] Department of Health, 'Clinical Negligence: What Are the Issues and Options for Reform?' 29 July 2003, available on the departmental website: www.doh.gov.uk.

[46] At paras 10 and 11.

[47] National Audit Office, 'Ministry of Defence: Compensation Claims', HC 957 (2002–3).

judiciary.[48] Audit is valuable in providing some empirical evidence about the cost of compensation. Its primary purpose is, however, as a managerial tool. It may sometimes produce surprising or unexpected information, as in the case of the report into the MoD. Occasionally, as with the DoH report, a wider debate may be stimulated. Medical mishap is, however, a special area, in which no-fault compensation has been on the agenda for many years; it is by no means clear that similar soul-searching inside the MoD would be helpful. A number of class claims, such as the Gulf War Veterans' claim, are currently under consideration and included in the statistical forecast. Perhaps these could form the basis for a wider inquiry into compensation practice and contribute to the debate over state liability and the search for a general principle of compensation.

Perhaps the next area for NAO attention should be the police. We know that the police pay out large sums in settlement of threatened actions: in 2001–2, for example, settlements cost the Metropolitan Police alone £776,000. The fact that a total of £1.25 million in court awards is also listed[49] suggests that settlement of liability rather than compensation is in issue. That is, however, almost the sum total of what we know. Amongst pressing questions to which answers might be given are: Which of the awards made by police authorities cover traffic accidents? Which are settlements and how are settlements handled? What sum represents exemplary damages and what, if any, changes have we seen after the Court of Appeal laid down new and more restrictive guidelines in 1998?[50] The problem with the

---

[48] In *Heil v Rankin* [2000] 2 WLR 1173, following the report of the Law Commission, 'Report on Damages for Personal Injury: Non-Pecuniary Loss', Law Com No 257 (1999), the Court of Appeal, sitting in a special formation and allowing interventions from leading insurers, moved to allow substantial increases in the level of damages. See also *Wells v Wells* [1999] 1 AC 345.

[49] The Annual Reports of the Metropolitan Police Service contain figures but these are hard to interpret: the AR for 2001–2 at 19 tells us, e.g., that claims declined from 1,500 in 1995–6 to 596 in 2001–2, with a cost in 1995 of £1,250,000 in court awards and £7,760,000 in settled actions. A figure of £4,850,000 is given for 'threatened actions'.

[50] *Thompson v Commissioner of Metropolitan Police* [1998] QB 498.

opaque and frustrating figures, in any case fragmented as police forces are not centralized, relates less to the need for administrative compensation than to accountability. The public has never accepted the system of police complaints as wholly satisfactory and it does not, in any event, make provision for compensation, a deliberate omission that has brought much resentment.[51] A detailed breakdown of the sums involved in settlement would at the very least be helpful in dispelling fears that informal, negotiatory processes are being used to disarm complainants and cover up serious malpractice. The suspicion must be that settlement is often a way, especially in public order cases, of 'purchasing illegality'.

There are obvious disadvantages in a scatter-gun approach to accident compensation but there are also advantages, not the least of which is cost. Activities and services can also be the subject of in-depth research and rounded consideration, which only policy-makers can really accomplish. Personal injuries cases can be considered separately from issues of property and economic loss. After all, a start has always to be made somewhere and, in time, we can hope to see islands of compensation joined and consolidated, much as the negligence principle has operated within the civil law to join peninsulas of liability and eliminate islands of immunity.

### COMPENSATION AS GOOD ADMINISTRATION

The principles of good administration observed by modern public services, trained to see themselves as caring and responsive, normally include some form of compensation principle. This may be used, as already indicated, to deal either with individual cases or as a short-term solution for a crisis situation or other specific problem. A decade ago, the

---

[51] For an outline of the police complaints system see Harlow and Rawlings, above note 4, at 414–21. R. Clayton and H. Tomlinson, *Civil Actions against the Police* (3rd edn, London, Sweet and Maxwell, 2003) provides a comprehensive account of remedies against the police.

select committee on the Parliamentary Commissioner for Administration (PCA), primed by Sir William Reid, then PCA, expressed its displeasure at 'the inadequacy of much of the redress offered by departments and agencies, [their] unwillingness to admit fault, refusal to identify and gracefully compensate those affected by acts of maladministration'.[52] They were dissatisfied too with the haphazard way in which *ex gratia* compensation was administered, and demanded a 'thematic inquiry'. A subsequent review by the PCA[53] echoed the dissatisfaction. A surprising number of compensation schemes came to light, varying in size and scale, some statutory in origin, others *ex gratia*, many entirely unpublicized; many anomalies and substantial differences of practice were also revealed. Rejecting Treasury Guidelines as 'frequently inappropriate' and its advice as 'outdated, restrictive and doctrinaire', the PCA took the view that compensation should be made in all cases of 'abnormal hardship' caused by maladministration. The select committee was prepared to be yet more generous with taxpayers' money, demanding a principle of full restitution: that 'a person who has suffered injury as a result of maladministration should be put back in the same position as he or she would have been in had things gone right in the first place'.[54] A similar line is followed in Guidance issued subsequently by the Commission for Local Administration,[55] which also states that someone affected by maladministration should be 'put back in the same position as he or she would have been in had things gone right in the first place'.

In addition, the PCA called for what he called 'botheration payments' to be routinely awarded to cover cases of grave maladministration, where excessive rudeness and malice were involved or exceptional worry and distress

[52] Third Report of the Select Committee on the PCA, HC 345 (1993–4).
[53] Parliamentary Commissioner for Administration, *Maladministration and Redress*, HC 112 (1994–5).
[54] Ibid.
[55] Commission for Local Administration, 'Guidance on Good Practice: 6. Remedies', available on the CLA website: www.lgo.org.uk

caused. One may instance in this context a notorious case where the Child Support Agency sent a maintenance inquiry form to the wrong individual, causing quite unnecessary anxiety and fomenting marital discord. This situation lasted over a period of some eleven weeks, during which the CSA failed either to apologize or rectify the error. In this situation, apologies did not, in the view of the PCA, provide adequate redress for the calumny and he recommended financial compensation as more appropriate.[56] This terminology of 'botheration payments' nicely captures the idea of affront to human dignity, fast becoming a fashionable human rights value.[57] A similar idea was once expressed by Ogus, who advanced the notion of 'demoralization costs', which he thought should be paid by the state to reflect 'the degree of resentment or outrage suffered by individuals subjected to pervasive incursions into their individual autonomy'.[58] 'Botheration payments' might be helpful in settling the queasy stomach of the Law Commission in its rather muddled discussion of aggravated damages, which it hopes to replace with the open-ended concept of 'damages for mental distress'[59]—a concept that has surely caused enough 'botheration' already.

One case handled by the PCA is of particular interest for providing a direct comparison with the tort action.[60] In the course of its regulatory duties, the Department of Transport and its agent, the Marine Safety Agency, had wrongly certified a fishing boat as seaworthy. The finding was accepted by the complainants' valuers without further investigation, with the consequence that they purchased from the vendor

---

[56] Case No C.31/94, HC 135 (1995–6) at 13, 14.

[57] Feldman, 'Human Dignity as a Legal Value' [1999] *PL* 682. And see the European Charter of Fundamental Rights, Final [2000] OJ C364-1, (18 December 2000).

[58] A. Ogus, 'Do We Have a General Theory of Compensation? [1984] *Current Legal Problems* 29, 37.

[59] Law Commission, 'Aggravated, Exemplary and Restitutionary Damages', Law Com No 247 (1997) paras 2.39–2.42.

[60] Case C557/98, First Report of the PCA, HC 20 (2001–2), further discussed by P. Giddings, 'Regulators, Contracts and Ombudsmen' (unpublished paper presented to EGPA, Lisbon, September 2003) to whom I owe the reference.

at too high a price. After investigation, the PCA drew the conclusion that there had been a breakdown of the certification system operated by the DoT and that this amounted to maladministration causing injustice to the purchasers. This is a point of some interest in that, in previous litigation, the Court of Appeal had, with some reluctance, ruled against the existence of a duty of care.[61] The PCA was prepared to go deeper and wider than the Court, recommending substantial compensation. After negotiation, this was fixed at the considerable sum of £750,000 for loss of the vessel, which had foundered, and loss of livelihood. To this the PCA added ancillary financial loss in the shape of bank charges, consequential repossession of the complainants' house, surrender of their pension investments and insurance policies to meet their debts, consultant's fees, and legal costs incurred in the unsuccessful negligence action. All this was justified by a reference to the 'exceptional circumstances' and to the degree of distress and trauma caused by the maladministration.

Surely this act of bounty must raise the question whether these losses were truly 'abnormal'? Or did the PCA (Mr Buckley) stray outside the guidelines suggested by his predecessor (Sir William Reid)? A more appropriate and professional approach might have required construction of a rudimentary profit-and-loss account, to reflect the degree of risk normally accepted in a commercial venture by fishermen, bearing in mind that the boat was 'of modest value' in the scheme of things and its owners people of modest means. By allowing the compensation principle to veer too

---

[61] *Reeman v Department of Transport and Others* [1997] 2 Lloyds Rep 648. The court relied on *Marc Rich and Co v Bishop Rock Marine Co Ltd* [1995] 3 WLR 227, which concerned a self-regulatory safety agency. Possibly the more appropriate precedent would have been *Smith v Eric Bush, Harris v Wyre Forest District Council* [1995] 1 AC 831, where surveyors were held to owe a duty of care to the purchasers of a house 'of modest value' on the ground that the surveyor understood that there would probably be reliance on his survey. However, the case failed on the issue of proximity: the inspection had been conducted for the previous owners, to whom any duty would have been owed.

far towards the principle of total restitution, a further serious escalation of state responsibility could be provoked.

It is not the primary purpose of the ombudsman system in this county to handle group complaints, and in practice it does so only occasionally and often at the request of government. One such occasion was, however, provided by the notorious Barlow Clowes affair, where investors lost large sums of money after fraudulent financial advisers went bankrupt.[62] A public inquiry set up by the government to investigate the conduct of the Department of Trade, which exercised functions of supervision and oversight in the area, found a measure of maladministration. The government, however, stubbornly refused to compensate. The matter was then referred by a group of angry constituency MPs to the PCA, who, in a hostile report, made a finding of maladministration causing injustice. This finding was hotly denied by the government, a point of interest being that it nonetheless agreed to compensate. It was expressly stated in the House of Commons that payments to investors, finally totalling £150 million, were to be made 'out of respect for the office of Parliamentary Commissioner'. This is not the first time that it has been demonstrated that ombudsmen can reach parts that other actors cannot reach.

## DAMAGES, HUMAN RIGHTS, AND COMPENSATION

A compensation principle could, however, provide an escape route for judges faced with claims for damages in the course of their new human rights jurisdiction. The wording of the Human Rights Act (HRA) creates serious ambiguity.[63] In addition to the 'declaration of incompatibility', the novel remedy peculiar to the Act, further

---

[62] R. Gregory and G. Drewry, 'Barlow Clowes and the Ombudsman' [1991] *PL* 192 and 408. And see Special Report of the PCA, 'The Barlow Clowes Affair' HC 76 (1989–90).

[63] The intended scope of the section was debated at length during passage of the Bill in the House of Lords: see HL Debs (Series 5) vols 582, 583, cols 825, 466.

remedies are foreseen. Section 8(1) of the Act permits the
court to grant 'such relief or remedy . . . within its powers as
it considers just and appropriate'. This section seems rather
to preserve the existing order than extend it, an interpretation quickly confirmed by section 8(2), which provides
that 'damages may be awarded only by a court which has
power to award damages, or to order the payment of compensation, in civil proceedings'. The intended effect
appears to be once more to tie pecuniary remedies in respect of the 'unlawful act of a public authority' firmly to
'civil proceedings'. The link is, however, severed by the
next subsections: according to section 8(3)(b), no award of
damages is to be made unless the court is satisfied in all the
circumstances that 'the award is necessary to afford *just
satisfaction* to the person in whose favour it is made'; section
8(4) refers more specifically to the practice of the Strasbourg
Court by providing that the courts must, in determining
whether to award *damages* and what the amount of *damages*
should be, 'take into account the principles applied by the
ECtHR in relation to the award of *compensation* under Article 41 of the Convention'. By linking damages and compensation in this fashion, the Act has left a valuable loophole for
our courts.

In a lecture given before Human Rights Act came into
force, Lord Woolf expressed the hope that the Act would
become a catalyst for change; distinctions between public
and private law remedies should be eliminated and remedies for the infringement of human rights and other unlawful
activities of public bodies should be as far as possible har-
monized.[64] Lord Woolf took the opportunity to warn
against an explosion of damages, on the ground that:[65]

The days when public bodies could be regarded as having purses
of bottomless depth are now past. An award of damages against a

---

[64] Lord Woolf, 'The Human Rights Act and Remedies' in M. Andenas
and D. Fairgrieve (eds), *Judicial Review in an International Perspective*
(London: Kluwer Law International, 2000) at 430. This lecture was cited
as authoritative guidance by the Law Commission, 'Damages Under The
Human Rights Act 1998', Law Com No 266 (2000) at 4.31.
[65] Lord Woolf, above note 64, at 433; Law Com No 266 at 4.33.

Health Authority can reduce the resources available for treating patients. An award against a Housing Authority can reduce the funds available for providing or repairing homes. There can be numerous victims of the same unlawful act.

Damages in human rights cases were by no means one and the same as tort damages and ought therefore to be 'on the low side with regard to awards in tort cases'. No greater sum should be awarded than is necessary to achieve 'just satisfaction', with a bar on exemplary or aggravated damages. Lord Woolf sketched out seven principles for the award of damages in human rights cases:[66]

1. Alternative redress. If there is any other appropriate remedy, it should take priority and there should be no automatic right to compensation.
2. No exemplary or aggravated damages.
3. The award should be no greater than necessary to achieve just satisfaction.
4. Damages should be moderate. They should not exceed analogous awards in tort cases and should normally be 'on the low side' by comparison with tort.
5. The award should reflect the degree of unlawfulness.
6. The claimant's own conduct could affect the award.
7. Pecuniary and non-pecuniary loss should not be distinguished: what counts is the claimant's 'real loss'.

Not all these requirements are free from ambiguity nor is the approach as a whole free from difficulty when a violation of human rights replicates or substantially overlaps with a well-established tort. Not only does it involve departure from the normal tort law rule of full restitution,[67] but also it carries the unfortunate implication that human rights rate less highly with the judiciary than the 'ordinary' law of torts. This is an inference judges are naturally reluctant to see drawn, and one which may be said to place them in something of a 'decision trap'. The predicament undoubtedly weighed heavily with one judge recently hearing

[66] Lord Woolf, above note 64, at 434.
[67] As noted by the Law Commission, above note 64, at 4.61.

an action where Mental Health Review Tribunals in hearing applications had subjected patients to undue delay, resulting in some cases in prolongation of detention. Equating the situation with injury suffered through false imprisonment, Stanley Burnton J awarded damages on a similar basis.[68] In another case of damages under the Human Rights Act,[69] we find a commendable piece of lateral thinking. The claimant, severely disabled and with a large family, had asked the council for housing appropriate to her condition. The council properly took responsibility but, through operational negligence, left the claimant and her family to suffer conditions of squalor, while nearly two years of litigation, delay, failure to carry out statutory duties, and distressing administrative incompetence elapsed.[70] Finally, the claimant's solicitors lost patience and asked for damages under the Human Rights Act, claiming in addition to the obvious breach of the right to private and family life (ECHR Article 8) that the conditions suffered had been degrading (ECHR Article 3).[71] In view of the long period spent by the family in 'deplorable conditions, wholly inimical to any normal family life' and taking into consideration also the absence of explanation or apology, merely to re-house the family in appropriate accommodation—as had by the time of trial been arranged— was unsatisfactory; Sullivan J, the trial judge, insisted that

---

[68] *R (KB and others) v Mental Health Review Tribunal and Health Secretary* [2003] EWHC 193 (Stanley Burnton J). Arguably, the analogy is a false one, as trespass is a tort of intention, while a delayed hearing is the product (at worst) of negligence or omission and results only in loss of a chance. This point is treated at paras 62–9. But see my views on *Doe v Metropolitan Toronto Board of Commissioners of Police* and *Simpson v AG* in Chap. 2 at note 120.

[69] *R (Bernard) v Enfield LBC* [2002] EWHC 2282 (Sullivan J).

[70] It is difficult to disentangle the complicated series of unfortunate events, but the case had been preceded by an unsuccessful application for judicial review of the council's decision that the applicants had rendered themselves 'intentionally homeless' and may thus have made an attempt at 'collateral review': see further *Bernard v Enfield LBC* [2001] EWCA Civ 2717.

[71] The Art 3 claim was dismissed, as the judge ruled that the 'minimum threshold of severity' had not been crossed: see paras 26–31. The case therefore proceeded as a violation of Art 8.

an award of damages was also necessary. Feeding back into the case law the Guidance and practice of the Local Government Ombudsman in awarding compensation, the judge awarded a sum of £10,000[72]—in the circumstances, aptly termed a 'botheration payment'.

After these lectures were completed, the Court of Appeal made an important ruling in *Anufrijeva*,[73] blocking up three claims for damages under ECHR Article 8 (right to private and family life). All three of the claims were based on failure or omission. Two cases involved delay and general maladministration in the handling of asylum applications, leading in one case to prolonged separation. A's claim was different. It was based on failure to supply accommodation adequate for the infirm and elderly relative of an asylum-seeker. This raises the question whether the compensation represented actual loss or falls into Cane and Atiyah's third category of compensation for 'what the victim has never had in comparison with others in a similar situation'.[74]

In a single judgment delivered for the court by Lord Woolf CJ, a strong Court of Appeal disallowed the claims. They ruled that, save in exceptional circumstances, Article 8 creates no general obligation to provide financial assistance: its positive obligations stop short at requiring (i) that an appropriate statutory or administrative scheme is in place to ensure that private and family life is protected, together with (ii) that the scheme is sufficiently competently operated for it to achieve its aim. Thus, while error of judgement, inefficiency, or maladministration occurring in the purported performance of a statutory duty could amount in principle to a breach of Article 8, it would be rare in practice for maladministration to be regarded as a violation. There must, in Lord Woolf's view, be 'an element of culpability. At the very least, there must be knowledge that the

---

[72] At para 61. At paras 59–60, Sullivan J comments that damages awarded by courts for pain and suffering appear to fall below the practice of the ombudsman.
[73] *Anufrijeva v Southwark LBC* [2003] EWCA Civ 406 (Lord Woolf CJ, Lord Phillips MR and Auld LJ).
[74] Cane and Atiyah, above note 6, at 402.

claimant's private and family life were at risk'.[75] This judgment marks something of a breakthrough, making it easier
for judges to draw appropriate bright-lines.

For the first time, the Court of Appeal in *Anufrijeva* drew
a distinction between 'damages' in a tort action and under
the HRA. The confusing formula of the Human Rights
Act was interpreted so as to acknowledge 'the different
role played by damages in human rights litigation to the
award of damages in a private law contract or tort action'.[76]
A tentative bright-line was also drawn between 'liability'
and 'compensation'[77] not only in human rights cases but
also in European Union law. The Court felt that an 'equitable' approach should be adopted and confirmed the
analogy with maladministration, by approving the use of
ombudsman awards as affording an appropriate compara-
tor.[78] Reiterating his earlier Guidance, Lord Woolf stressed
the *discretionary* nature of compensation in Human Rights
Act cases, where damages are not, as in civil law, an automatic entitlement but a remedy of last resort. In considering
whether it was just and appropriate to award compensation, courts were therefore entitled to consider not only the
circumstances of the individual victim but also what would
serve the interests of the 'wider public who have an interest
in the continued funding of a public service'.

Still more significant were the Court's procedural recommendations, which seek to reinstate the traditional common
law 'pecking order' of public law remedies by insisting that
Convention cases be channelled wherever possible through
judicial review procedure. Thus the judgment downplays
the damages as a remedy in HRA cases. The main concern
in a human rights application is, according to Lord Woolf,
*illegality*. The application seeks primarily:[79]

---

[75] Paras 41(7) and 45.     [76] Ibid.     [77] At paras 49 and 53.
[78] At paras 66, 74.
[79] At paras 52–53 (emphasis mine). The reasoning harks back to Lord
Woolf, 'Public Law—Private Law: Why the Divide? A Personal View'
[1986] *PL* 220 and *Protection of the Public—A New Challenge*, The Hamlyn
Lectures (London: Stevens, 1990). It reinstates a flexible public/private
boundary, as argued for in C. Harlow, 'Why Public Law is Private Law:
An Invitation to Lord Woolf' in R. Cranston and A. Zuckerman (eds), *The
Woolf Report Reviewed* (Oxford: Clarendon Press, 1995).

to bring the infringement to an end and any question of compensation will be of secondary, if any, importance. This is reflected in the fact that, when it is necessary to resort to the courts to uphold and protect human rights, the remedies that are most frequently sought are the orders which are the descendents of the historic prerogative orders or declaratory judgments. The orders enable the court to order a public body to refrain from or to take action, or to quash an offending administrative decision of a public body. Declaratory judgments usually resolve disputes as to what is the correct answer in law to a dispute. *This means that it is often procedurally convenient for actions concerning human rights to be heard on an application for judicial review in the Administrative Court.* That court does not normally concern itself with issues of disputed fact or with issues as to damages. However, it is well placed to take action expeditiously when this is appropriate.

Judges considering human rights claims were warned to look first to alternative remedies, in particular to investigation by an ombudsman or mediation.[80]

Is there a hint here that the Administrative Court might be a court with power 'to order the payment of compensation'? In my view, it should be. Order 53, which updated judicial review procedure, tied damages and tort law indissolubly, by providing that damages can be awarded on an application for judicial review only where they *could also have been awarded in an action begun by writ.*[81] The power has in any case been exercised very sparingly, the preference of the

---

[80] At para 8: courts 'should look critically at' attempts to recover damages under the Human Rights Act in any manner other than judicial review. In advising resort to mediation, the Court of Appeal is following the practice recommended by Lord Woolf CJ in *R (Cowl) v Plymouth City Council (Practice Note)* [2002] 1 WLR 803, a case which seeks to contain the flood of cases challenging closure of old people's homes after it had been decided in *R v North and East Devon Health Authority ex p Coughlan* [2000] 2 WLR 622 that a substantive 'legitimate expectation' could in certain circumstances be created such as to prevent closure. It is questionable whether this advice would satisfy the ECtHR's requirements under ECHR Art 13 and Art 6(1).

[81] RSC Order 53, implemented by SI 1955 No 1977. The matter is now governed by s. 31(4) of the Supreme Court Act 1981 and RSC Part 54 Rule 3(2), which provides that a claim for judicial review may include a claim for damages but may not seek damages alone. The best account is Part 19 of de Smith, Woolf, and Jowell, *Judicial Review of Administrative Action* (5th edn, London: Sweet and Maxwell, 1995).

Administrative Court being to transfer damages claims to the High Court to be heard by writ. This preference is understandable: damages actions are complex and judicial review procedures unsuitable for hearing evidence and for complex fact-finding. The formula of the Human Rights Act, which provides for the award of damages 'only by a court with power to award damages, or to order the payment of compensation',[82] preserves the traditional link. All that is needed is a marginal adjustment to judicial review procedure to entrust the Administrative Court with power, in exceptional cases, to make an award of *compensation*: in short, to endow that prestigious court—at least on an experimental basis—with an *equitable* jurisdiction to act in exceptional cases of *abnormal* loss or *exceptional* hardship or *grave* violation of human rights as government, administrators, and ombudsmen already do. No doubt the temptation to make 'botheration payments' would prevail on occasion!

### TOWARDS A GENERAL PRINCIPLE?

Should we be moving towards a general principle of compensation? Cane certainly thinks so. In an ambitious exploration of the subject, Cane bases his argument on two assumptions, reflecting the division of power in democratic societies:

- first, government is entitled to use state programmes for the redistribution of resources;
- secondly, those made worse off by the lawful operation of legitimate schemes have no automatic entitlement to compensation.[83]

Broadly, Cane recognizes the legitimacy of a distributive justice function and sees the function as legitimately vested

---

[82] S. 8(2) and 8(4) of the Human Rights Act 1988, above, text at note 63.
[83] P. Cane, 'Damages in Public Law' (1999) 9 *Univ. of Otago L Rev.* 489, 497–8. Cane calls these victims 'endogenous losers' and contrasts them with 'exogenous losers', who are those affected by 'illegitimate features' of a scheme. I have preferred to avoid this terminology.

in government and legislature. He agrees that legitimate policies should be respected so long as they are carried through legitimately. But governments, Cane argues, should not be free to ignore with impunity 'the constraints imposed on them by their citizens'. From this he deduces that someone who is 'made worse off by the operation of an illegitimate feature of a government programme' is entitled to be compensated. Compensation is a necessary corrective to restore equilibrium and, without it, the 'legitimacy of government' is imperilled. Thus Cane draws his bright-line between 'legitimate' and 'illegitimate' acts, a distinction which, if I have understood him correctly, mirrors the lawful/unlawful bright-line of classical administrative law. He seems to be re-opening an earlier debate over liability for illegal or invalid administrative acts[84] and using his compensation principle to resolve it. According to Cane's theory, losses would be left uncompensated only if attributable to a legitimate government programme executed in a legitimate fashion. Cane's principle points to compensation in *Bernard* and *Anufrijeva*, both involving legitimate but badly executed schemes.

By tying compensation so closely to liability, Cane's approach leaves many unresolved problems. Is he, for example, advocating strict or no-fault liability for unlawful government action, perhaps with the motive of using damages to control abuse of power? If so, his theory comes near to admitting that all loss resulting from illegitimate administrative action should fall on the state—a dangerously wide form of risk liability, which requires of the state that its plans and services should be infallible—or else! Administration, in other words, acts 'at its risks and perils' and carries the risk of failure in the enterprise of governance.[85] This is an outcome that would play havoc with public

---

[84] See e.g., B. Gould, 'Damages as a Remedy in Administrative Law' [1972] *New Zealand Univ. LR* 105; 14th Report of the Public and Administrative Law Reform Committee, *Damages in Administrative Law* (Wellington, New Zealand, 1980).

[85] Harlow, above note 1, at 100 and, more generally, 87–101. The idea was firmly rejected by the Privy Council (in my view rightly) in *Dunlop v Woollahara Municipal Council* [1981] 2 WLR 693.

finance, too perilous for any court or any government to contemplate. Since, on the other hand, Cane's compensation principle does not contemplate payment of compensation where loss is caused by state action that is legitimate, it cannot easily extend to loss, however catastrophic, flowing from primary legislation,[86] though reference to 'the constraints imposed by citizens' could perhaps encompass violations of human rights or other constitutional norms.[87]

A more targeted and specific principle, appropriate to redistributive welfare services, is the concept of 'entitlement' used by Cohen and Smith to ground a theory of state liability. According to this theory, citizens possess 'positive entitlements' to benefits from state programmes, provided they fall within the scheme's parameters. If 'by inadvertence individuals fail to receive that to which they are entitled, they should have recourse to the law against the state or the relevant public body as a matter of public entitlement'.[88] Citizens also possess 'negative rights', which are rights of non-interference, giving rise to liability if violated, to cover cases of property requisition and planning compensation. Unlike some principles of distributive justice, this one is serviceable because it contains its own control devices. The principle transcends the legal/illegal boundary and can extend to cases involving no illegality: it might, for example, be applied so as to permit compensation in a case where the applicant could show entitlement but no public housing was available.

It is helpful to test the operation of the entitlement principle against a case which, not long ago, gave the House of Lords some difficulty.[89] O'Rourke had been

---

[86] I deliberately leave out of account the question of liability under EU law, covered by *Francovich* and classified, as indicated earlier, by Lord Woolf in *Anufrijeva* as compensation.

[87] Along the lines of the German *Schutznormtheorie*: above, Chap. 2 at note 58.

[88] D. Cohen and J. Smith, 'Entitlement and the Body Politic: Rethinking Negligence in Public Law' (1986) 64 *Can. Bar Rev.* 1, 12.

[89] *O'Rourke v Camden LBC* [1997] 3 WLR 86. The House ruled that a 'public law decision' was challengeable only through judicial review,

placed in temporary accommodation pending a final decision on his entitlement to public housing in terms of the Housing (Homeless Persons) Act 1977. For some reason not made entirely clear, he was evicted and, in the absence of resources, had to sleep rough. He claimed damages, to which the House of Lords ruled he was not entitled. I want to focus on a passage where Lord Hoffmann describes the housing programme as a social welfare scheme, 'intended to confer benefits at the *public* expense on grounds of *public* policy'—a passage in which, incidentally, the word 'public' recurs so many times as to become virtually a conventional adjective:[90]

*Public* money is spent on housing the homeless not merely for the private benefit of people who find themselves homeless but on grounds of general *public interest*: because, for example, proper housing means that people will be less likely to suffer illness, turn to crime or require the attention of other social services. The expenditure interacts with expenditure on other *public* services such as education, the National Health Service and even the police. It is not simply a private matter between the claimant and the housing authority. Accordingly, the fact that Parliament has provided for the expenditure of *public money* on benefits in kind such as housing the homeless does not necessarily mean that it intended cash payments to be made by way of damages to persons who, in breach of the housing authority's statutory duty, have unfortunately not received the benefits which they should have done.

This type of reasoning often gives rise to criticism of the judiciary as parsimonious with public funds. But is Lord Hoffmann not expressing an aggregative view of public services? Perhaps ironically, he also seems to be approving the idea of 'collective consumption' that finds expression in an undeservedly disregarded lecture by McAuslan, who

applying the 'exclusive jurisdiction' rule established by *O'Reilly v Mackman* [1983] 2 AC 237 and *Cocks v Thanet RDC* [1983] 2 AC 286: see Sir Robert Carnwath, 'The *Thornton* Heresy Exposed: Financial Remedies for Breach of Public Duties' [1998] *PL* 407. An application to the ECtHR has since been held inadmissible.

[90] [1997] 3 WLR at 94 (emphasis mine).

criticizes the tendency of the judiciary to lean towards individualistic solutions.[91]

But why should the public nature of the housing service lead to the conclusion that public money should not be spent in compensating individuals? After all, it often is! And sleeping rough is hardly a matter either of public benefit or of private choice; it is likely to impinge on the NHS, the police, and even the public. An alternative explanation is to be found in Cohen and Smith's entitlement principle. This too would see housing the homeless as a public service but with redistributive characteristics. Where a particular individual like O'Rourke suffers loss through wrongful operation of the scheme, so the reasoning would run, an award of compensation is perfectly designed to achieve precisely the measure of distributive justice intended by the legislator. The effect on resources is no more and no less than if the claimant had been given his due in the first place, the only proviso being that damages shall not extend beyond what could have been obtained under the housing scheme. The wider outreach of the principle, however, remains perilously uncertain. How does it apply, for example, to cases, such as a schoolchild's entitlement to a SEN diagnosis, considered earlier?[92] Compensation is probably suggested. And what is its application to human rights cases, such as the right to special disability accommodation in *Bernard* and *Anufrijeva* or other welfare situations that currently puzzle the judges? And why does Cohen, who is much concerned with collective and aggregative values,[93] come down so firmly in favour of compensation as distributive justice?

In the *Bernard* case, where a 'botheration payment' seemed amply justified, the judge played down the danger of a 'compensation culture', presenting the classic case for sanction and deterrence:[94]

---

[91] P. McAuslan, 'Administrative Law, Collective Consumption and Judicial Policy' (1983) 46 *MLR* 1.

[92] *Phelps v Hillingdon LBC* [2001] 2 AC 619. And see above Chap. 2 at note 139.

[93] See especially Cohen, above note 11.

[94] *R (Bernard) v Enfield LBC* [2002] EWHC Civ 2282 at para 39.

I accept that in many cases the finding of a violation, particularly when coupled with a mandatory order, may constitute just satisfaction. Concerns have been expressed in various quarters about the development of a 'compensation culture'. In my experience in this court, dealing with a wide range of complaints against public authorities, most citizens who have suffered as a result of some bureaucratic error are not motivated, or at least not primarily motivated, by a desire for monetary compensation. They institute proceedings because they feel outraged by what they see as an injustice and want 'them', the faceless persons in an apparently insensitive, unresponsive and impenetrable bureaucratic labyrinth, to acknowledge that something has gone wrong, to provide them with an explanation, an apology and an assurance that steps have been taken to ensure (so far as possible in an imperfect world) that the same mistake will not happen again. This assurance will at least give them the satisfaction of knowing that they have not suffered in vain.

All those who witness with irritation and often outrage the effects of administrative error and ineffectiveness will have much sympathy with this justification of the corrective justice paradigm.

On the other hand, in denying the growth of a 'compensation culture' Sullivan J was unduly optimistic. What we are witnessing in the field of compensation is an extension of Atiyah's process of 'selective comparison'.[95] Extensions of legal liability stoke demands for compensation, which in turn fuel demands for greater compensation and expansion of legal liability. The circular process is neatly illustrated by events following the investigation into organ retention of infant children at Alder Hey hospital between the years 1988 and 1995.[96] In the wake of the investigation, bereaved relatives were granted generous compensation. A fund of £5 million provided around £5,000 in individual cases, in what was misleadingly called an out-of-court settlement. The immediate response was the foundation of the Nationwide Organ Retention Group to campaign for compensa-

---

[95] P. S. Atiyah, *The Damages Lottery* (Oxford: Hart Publishing, 1997), further discussed in Chap. 1.
[96] Report of the Royal Liverpool Children's Inquiry, available at www.rlcinquiry.org.uk

tion for other parents, affected by similar behaviour in other hospitals. Again, *ex gratia* compensation was offered, this time to twice as many families. The Group, dissatisfied with the sums offered in compensation, turned to an action in damages.[97] Here we have a clear manifestation of the compensation culture.

For this amongst other reasons, I believe that the many hard choices involved in compensation are best left to government and legislatures. Legislators remain the *legitimate* arbiters between collective and individual interests where resources are in issue; administrators are best placed to calculate financial implications and take corrective action, though always under the ultimate supervision of courts and ombudsmen. Ombudsmen are often underrated by lawyers because their recommendations lack binding force.[98] This is not necessarily a disadvantage; access to the administration combines with inquisitorial procedure to favour negotiated outcomes.[99] Ombudsman recommendations are usually taken very seriously[100] and ombudsmen can require a general rectification of systems that have given rise to a maladministration finding (and sometimes of those that do not).[101] They are also well placed to monitor compliance, which courts are not equipped to do. This is by and large a better accountability system than tort law can offer.

---

[97] *The Times*, 27 January 2004. At the time of writing, the outcome was unknown.

[98] See *Leander v Sweden* (1987) 9 EHRR 433 at paras 81–82.

[99] Harlow and Rawlings, above note 4, at 432–4.

[100] For PCA recommendations to be rejected is rare indeed, though see 'The Channel Tunnel Link and Blight: Investigation of Complaints against the Department of Transport', HC 193 (1994–5), where the DoT refused to extend the statutory compensation scheme in planning cases to long-term planning blight caused by inability to map the course of the Anglo-French line through Kent. In view of what has just been said, it is interesting to note the justification of the Permanent Secretary at the DoT that the concession would involve a general ratcheting-up of the legislation to cover similar cases. The argument is more often over failure by local authorities to respect ombudsman recommendations.

[101] Examples are cited in Harlow and Rawlings, above note 4, at 441–2.

With Cane, I see the need for a general principle of compensation to guide those who have to handle claims. This should clearly distinguish liability from compensation. As I have tried to demonstrate in this lecture, the basis for compensation is neither fault nor illegality. It may represent redress; it may, on the other hand, be merely a manifestation of sympathy and solace. I favour a simple and flexible principle narrowly interpreted to cover situations of 'abnormal loss' and hardship, with 'botheration payments' in appropriate cases.

# General Conclusion: Collective Consumption Reinstated

In these lectures, I have chosen to approach state liability through the classical tradition of tort law, though note has been taken throughout of semantic distinctions. These terminological differences did not, however, point in general to disenchantment with the judicial process: in the case of transnational jurisdictions, very much the reverse. In the second lecture, I have challenged the assumption that responsibility is synonymous with liability and that redress necessarily takes the form of compensation to individuals. The transnational courts, I noted, showed a marked preference for judicial process, rating it as more independent than redress through administrative or political authorities. In this context, I noted too the trend from negative to affirmative rights and remedies and the urge to cram into the judicial toolkit new and more intrusive remedies. The thrust of my argument was against these trends. In my final lecture, I questioned these conclusions, arguing that compensation is not only a legitimate dimension of policy-making but often a superior means of achieving justice. I supported the introduction of a general principle of compensation, applicable to cases of abnormal loss and damage, though with the caveat that compensation should not necessarily be equated with damages.

In the Introduction to these lectures, I signalled a significant shift from 'aggregative' to 'distributive' values, the former emphasizing collective responsibilities and group entitlements to public goods, the latter reflecting the personalized consumer values of the modern welfare state. It was in this context that Dawn Oliver first pointed to the

advance of 'security' as a *legal* value.[1] It had, she noted,
already crept across the boundary of physical integrity—
tort law's traditional heartland—to cover 'unwanted and
damaging change through loss of income, livelihood or
home'. This was a journey tort law too was making.[2] For
Oliver, security was a value meriting limited procedural
protection rather than a principle creating legally enforceable entitlements.[3] This restrictive interpretation was just
tenable when she wrote. Almost unnoticed, the compensation culture had already taken root, had sprouted, and
was soon to yield a fertile crop for tort lawyers. Security
quickly added to its credentials, drawing strength from
human rights discourse, as the case law of the Strasbourg
Court grafted on to the negative obligation entrenched in
the Convention its own affirmative conception of the right
to life, involving responsibility 'to take appropriate steps to
guard life'.[4] The evolution of this requirement was traced in
my second lecture as it transmuted into an embryonic *liability* principle, extended to inhuman treatment in *Z v United
Kingdom*,[5] while *Osman*[6] saw the first, admittedly tentative,
steps taken towards a right to security as 'a condition of
being protected from or not exposed to danger'.[7]

A risk-averse society was, I argued, being shaped, in
which a state of 'generalized reliance' on regulatory action
by government and on state programmes was developing
into a demand for a risk-free environment. Failures of

---

[1] D. Oliver, 'The Underlying Values of Public and Private Law' in M.
Taggart (ed), *The Province of Administrative Law* (Oxford: Hart Publishing,
1999) at 226.

[2] P. Cane, *Tort Law and Economic Interests* (Oxford: Clarendon, 1991).

[3] Oliver wrote before the doctrine of substantive legitimate expectation, an unfortunate example of the prioritization of distributive over
aggregative values, had been enunciated in *R v North and East Devon
Health Authority ex p Coughlan* [2000] 2 WLR 622. This case exacerbated
problems discussed in the previous lecture and led Lord Woolf to
express his preference for alternative dispute resolution: see Chap. 3 at
note 80.

[4] *X v United Kingdom*, Application No 7154/75 14 DR 31 (1978).

[5] *Z and others v United Kingdom* (2001) 34 EHRR 97.

[6] *Osman v United Kingdom* (1998) 29 EHRR 245.

[7] Oliver, above note 1.

regulation seemed then to point irrevocably to state responsibility, carrying correlative entitlements to compensation for individuals. This marked a transition to a belief in a form of distributive justice that was capable of embracing tort law as a distributive principle. In this context, Spigelman's provocative description of negligence as 'the last outpost of the welfare state'[8] could be read in two senses: on the one hand, in the sense apparently intended by the author, the liability system was being used to fill an increasing number of gaps in the distributive social services; on the other, it was increasingly seen as a welfare service in its own right.

I have no quarrel with social solidarity; it is a value to which, broadly speaking, I subscribe. Similarly, I am rather susceptible to the claims of distributive justice, in the broad sense of resource redistribution. All I am saying in these lectures is that these aspirations, however worthy, are inadequate as the foundations of a *liability system*. To make judgements about justice, Miller asserts, 'it is necessary to examine the relationships in which...beings stand to one another—for instance, by looking at the transactions in which they have engaged'.[9] This, corrective justice does. Unlike the focused doctrine of corrective justice, claims of distributive justice are not targeted. They do not tell us how to balance aggregative and distributive interests, nor do they contain adequate control devices for distinguishing the claims of individuals. Some sacrifices are acknowledged as justified in the public interest, but we are not told which or why. That is one reason why I have always opted for legislative choice in compensation questions.

Again, although this belief runs counter to that of many lawyers, in particular human rights lawyers, I believe very strongly that a 'public law damages culture' is undesirable. As I have tried to show, it has the inevitable effect of siphoning resources out of public services and perhaps— for the empirical evidence is simply not available—of

---

[8] J. J. Spigelman, 'Negligence: the Last Outpost of the Welfare State' (2002) 76 *ALJ* 432.

[9] D. Miller, *Social Justice* (Oxford: Clarendon, 1976) at 18.

fostering a timid and risk-averse public service. Only a strong belief in the deterrent properties of tort law could justify such an outcome, and only an economic rationalist could sincerely hold to a belief in tort law's deterrent properties. For this reason, I have advocated a shrinking tort law and a bright-line between compensation and legal liability. I see that this could be helpful in avoiding the ratcheting-up effect of tort damages on awards of compensation which, I have argued above, adds fuel to the blazing compensation culture. Similarly, that is why I cling to the belief that administrative compensation should extend only to 'abnormal' and 'exceptional' losses plus, in limited cases, 'botheration payments'.

I have always maintained the position that problems of state liability are really problems of tort law and that they cannot be resolved by special rules of 'public' liability. I have continued to maintain this position throughout these lectures, by arguing for less haphazard and indiscriminate expansion. What is required in my view is a more focused tort law, fitting comfortably into its corrective justice framework. Admittedly, this is a pronounced change of direction, calling for legislative intervention. I should like to see the matter referred to a small advisory committee with a highly specific agenda and a shorter time frame than that of the ill-fated Pearson Commission. There would be a need to think laterally about problems of resourcing, and especially the respective roles of insurance and government funding. Particular areas, such as liability and compensation in the NHS, might have to be hived off to task forces with specialized information. Just such a process has been undertaken in Australia,[10] in response to the collapse of two vast insurance companies, one handling more than 20 per cent of the public liability insurance market, the second, the largest medical indemnity insurer. The Ipp committee was asked to work in a time frame of around two months on limited

---

[10] *Review of the Law of Negligence* (The Ipp Review) (Canberra: Commonwealth of Australia) 2002. On an earlier US initiative by the Reagan Administration see D. Harris, 'Tort Law Reform in the United States' (1991) 11 *OJLS* 407.

terms of reference: to inquire into 'the application, effective-ness and operation' of common law principles in personal injuries cases and 'develop and evaluate principled options to limit liability and quantum of awards for damages'.[11]

Despite the unsatisfactory nature of some of the case law, Ipp saw no need for fundamental changes to the parity principle.[12] To the contrary, it wished to see substituted for the prevalent public/private distinction in the case law an activity-based approach. Thus in cases involving sporting and other recreational activity, where the law was supposedly having serious effects of 'negative deter-rence', Ipp recommended *against* liability on the part of providers of recreational services, at least where the victim was a voluntary participant in a recreational activity and the injury resulted as the materialization of an obvious risk.[13]

This activity-based approach would help to reconcile a number of confusing and unsatisfactory cases involving responsibility for recreational facilities, open spaces, and sporting activities, where public authorities seem to be be-coming less liable just as professional sporting bodies are becoming more liable. Is this a further manifestation of judicial concern over public funds? In *Tomlinson v Congleton BC*,[14] where a swimmer had foolishly dived into a shallow lake, a local authority as occupier just squeaked home with-out liability on the ground that adequate warning of danger had been given. Against this, a series of cases has sharply ratcheted up the liability of those offering, regulating, and, most recently, refereeing risky sports, notably rugby

---

[11] At ix.

[12] Ipp at 151–62 and Recommendation 142. A provision designed to prevent the use of an action based on statutory duty being used to circumvent limitations on negligence liability included in the implement-ing legislation was, however, recommended.

[13] Recommendation 11. Obvious risks are broadly defined. See also paras 4.1–4.19 and recommendations 10, 12.

[14] *Tomlinson v Congleton BC* [2003] 2 AC 1120. See also *Donoghue v Folkestone Properties* [2003] 2 WLR 1138 and *Romeo v Conservation Com-mission of the Northern Territory* (1998) 151 ALR 263, discussed with *Jolley v Sutton LBC* [2000] 1 WLR 1082, in Chap. 1 at notes 45, 46.

football and boxing.[15] The problem is that this is not an area for compulsory insurance, though in practice many such bodies are insured; the insurance position needs to be clear, yet the Court of Appeal has firmly resisted formally taking the insurance position into account.[16] Policy needs to be determined and consideration given to a broad range of issues: whether public and private schools, professional and amateur sporting bodies should be required to take out collective insurance; whether amateur sporting and recreational activities warrant a 'no liability' rule. More important, however, issues such as this need to be permanently on the agenda of government and 'benchmarked' for attention whenever, for example, Education Acts and education budgets are under review.

For public bodies, the Ipp committee suggested a 'policy defence', designed to protect 'policy decisions', a term of art which would cover decisions 'based substantially on financial, economic, political or social factors or constraints', except where the decision was 'so unreasonable that no reasonable *public functionary* in the defendant's position could have made it'.[17] Admittedly, this would settle the longstanding judicial argument over the relative weight of the public law standard of *Wednesbury* unreasonableness as against the more robust negligence test favoured by Lord Reid in *Dorset Yacht*.[18] I would personally favour more direct 'bad faith only' provisions, as found in many modern statutes, though I admit that in the long run

---

[15] *Van Oppen v Clerk to the Bedford Charity Referees* [1990] 1 WLR 235 (school liable to pupil for rugby accident); *Watson v British Boxing Board of Control* [2001] 2 WLR 1256 (BBBC liable to brain-damaged boxer for failure to put adequate regulations in place); *Vowles v Evans* [2003] 1 WLR 1607 (referee, hence his professional body vicariously, liable for accident in badly packed scrum).

[16] *Vowles v Evans* [2003] 1 WLR 1607. The fact that the referee was insured was known to both courts. See the note by J. Elvin (2003) 119 *LQR* 560, 561, stating that Vowles got £91,000 under cover provided by the Welsh Rugby Union to all member clubs.

[17] Recommendation 39 (emphasis mine).

[18] *Home Office v. Dorset Yacht Co. Ltd.* [1970] AC 1004, further discussed in Chap. 1.

this may be a distinction without much difference. I would also favour blocking up liability across the public/private divide. The so-called 'business judgement' rule, which requires corporate decision-makers to be 'reasonably informed' before making a decision, covers bad faith in the sense of conscious wrongdoing or dishonest purpose, but corporate business judgement may also be constructed out of corporate acts or inferred objectively where 'the decision is so far beyond the bounds of reasonable judgement that it seems essentially inexplicable on any ground other than bad faith'.[19] Perhaps the much maligned *Wednesbury* test is simply an objective bad faith standard, capable of application alike to public and private bodies.

A further change designed to tie public and private law more closely together concerns the public law tort of 'misfeasance in public office'. On the one hand, this should be expanded, as Lord Steyn has suggested, to cover all those 'in a position of corporate responsibility'. This would meet the point made by Lord Nicholls, speaking in another recent case, that national and international companies also exercise enormous power, making it wrong to exclude them from the reach of retribution by drawing bright-lines between 'the boardroom and the bureau'.[20] On the other hand, misfeasance should be confined to acts of 'targeted malice', in which wrongful conduct is intended to cause injury, or where unlawful action is taken in the knowledge that the actor acts outside the scope of his authority.[21] I believe that the law should mark malfeasance in the sense of real wrongdoing, as in cases of sexual abuse, or where police officers stand aside to watch citizens as-

---

[19] J. Beerman, 'Administrative-Law-Like Obligations on Privat[ized] Entities' 49 *UCLA L Rev.* 1717, 1725 (2002). See also S. Corcoran, 'Bad Faith and Bad Intentions in Corporate Law' in N. Naffine, R. Ownes, J. Williams (eds), *Intention in Law and Philosophy* (Ashgate: Dartmouth, 2001).

[20] *Kuddus v Chief Constable of Leicestershire Constabulary* [2001] 2 WLR 1789 at para 66.

[21] *Three Rivers DC v Bank of England (No 3)* [2000] 2 WLR 1220, 1231 (Lord Steyn). The paradigm cases will always be *Ashby v White* (1703) 14 St. Tr. 695 and *Roncarelli v Duplessis* (1959) 16 DLR (2d) 689.

saulted[22] or deliberate fraud and falsification are involved.[23] Exemplary damages may be appropriate for the rare cases in which the court wishes to register condemnation of outrageous conduct or mark the defendant's contumelious disregard of the plaintiff's rights, as in *Botrill's case*,[24] where it was held for this reason that an action for exemplary damages survives the extinction of personal injuries actions in the Accident Compensation Act. The test favoured by the New Zealand Court of Appeal was one of 'intentional wrongdoing and conscious recklessness'; unfortunately, however, it was softened in the Privy Council so as to cover cases where the defendant's conduct would be considered outrageous by the public so that condemnation was called for.[25] This test, which strays well outside the objectivity of the 'business judgement' rule is surely a most unreliable criterion for liability and opens the way for exemplary damages to be awarded in negligence cases, reopening and casting further doubt on the Camelford case,[26] an instance of near-intentional corporate wrongdoing where public condemnation was certainly not in doubt! The same rules should apply to institutions but only where the outrageous conduct is systematized or if those in authority are truly complicit in the activities of the primary actors.[27] But the law of exemplary damages is, as Lord Nicholls recently protested, yet another area that 'cries aloud for parliamentary intervention'[28] despite a Law Com-

[22] *R v Dytham* (1979) 2 QB 722; *Kuddus v Chief Constable of Leicestershire Constabulary* (above note 20).

[23] *Akenzua v Home Secretary* (2002) ECWA Civ 470, where a Jamaican national involved in drugs and violent crime was allowed to remain in the country as a police informer and later carried out a sexual murder.

[24] *Botrill v A* [2001] 3 NZLR 622 (an action for exemplary damages survives s. 319 of the Accident Compensation Act 2001, extinguishing personal injuries actions).

[25] *Botrill v A* [2003] 1 AC 449.

[26] *AB v South West Water Services* [1993] 1 All ER 609, already doubted in *Kuddus* (above): see Chap. 2 at note 24.

[27] *Lister v Hesely Health Authority* [2001] 2 WLR 1311, overriding *Trotman v N Yorks County Council* [1999] LGR 584, introduces vicarious liability in cases of sexual abuse.

[28] *Kuddus v Chief Constable of Leicestershire Constabulary* [2001] 2 WLR 1789 at para 60.

mission programme on the law of damages all awaiting implementation.[29]

There is a sharp contrast here with the Australian Ipp Report, a political initiative that caught the appropriate moment and has had the advantage of momentum. A recent codification of negligence law in New South Wales[30] has adopted the main proposals and further Commonwealth initiatives are on the cards. Here, parliamentary intervention seems unlikely. When will our legislators realize that tort law raises issues of great political and financial moment?

Tort law urgently needs a political steer and legislative input. Indeed, given the likely impact on resources, I find the lack of attention paid by policy-makers to compensation issues both culpable and surprising. Still more culpable is the lack of attention paid to the question by legislative draftsmen, a matter once taken up by the English Law Commission in the context of statutory duty. They recommended a rule of interpretation whereby every statutory duty should be presumed to be capable of giving rise to liability unless expressly excluded.[31] This recommendation, which might have wonderfully concentrated the minds of parliamentary draftsmen, unfortunately never saw the light of day. Whether it would have been enough to deter the customary guessing games of judges, I rather doubt, however.

If tort law is to retract, as I have suggested it should do, towards a residual position, a very positive legislative steer is necessary. Under the Human Rights Act, government ministers are obliged, when introducing new legislation, to draw the attention of the House to the compatibility or intentional incompatibility of the provisions with rights protected by the European Convention,[32] an obligation

---

[29] The relevant report is Law Commission, 'Aggravated, Exemplary and Restitutionary Damages', Law Com No 247 (1997).

[30] Civil Liability Amendment (Personal Responsibility) Act 2002 (NSW).

[31] Law Commission, *The Interpretation of Statutes*, Law Com No 21 (1969), Draft Clause 4.

[32] S. 19 of the Human Rights Act 1988.

which gives Parliament an opportunity expressly to consider important issues of human rights and seems to be taken relatively seriously by legal advisers and very seriously by the parliamentary Joint Committee on Human Rights. Again, impact assessment, a technique borrowed from Europe, is now the order of the day in environmental policy-making and is beginning to be diffused more widely. The Regulatory Impact Unit publishes guidance for policy-makers on how to carry out regulatory impact assessments and when this should be done.[33] In other sensitive areas, such as race and gender, 'benchmarking' is used to ensure that policy-makers bear these issues in mind.[34] As Hogg forcefully reminded the participants at the colloquium where my intellectual journey started, it ought to be a routine part of policy-making for planners to 'undertake an analysis of the private losses that might be caused' by every new government programme;[35] compensation and liability, in other words, should be 'benchmarked' as a standard drafting practice. This would force policy-makers to treat compensation issues seriously, encourage good drafting and ensure that the attention of the legislators was engaged. The onus would then lie squarely on Parliament to see express provision made for civil liability, obviating the various guessing games about legislative intention which have formed much of the subject-matter of these lectures.

[33] The Unit is set up within the Cabinet Office and the practice authorized by the Regulatory Reform Act 2001.

[34] F. Beveridge, *et al.*, 'Addressing Gender in the Nation and Community: Law and Policymaking' in J. Shaw (ed), *Social Law and Policy in an Evolving European Union* (Oxford: Hart Publishing, 2000).

[35] P. Hogg, 'Compensation for Damage Caused by Government' (1995) 6 *NJCL* 7, 12.

# Annex:
# State Liability and French
# Administrative Law

France owes its special administrative jurisdiction to a decision, taken at the time of the French Revolution and usually attributed to revolutionary impatience with the obstacles—justifiable or otherwise—set in the way of strong executive government by the obstructive *Parlements* of the Ancien Régime, to curtail the jurisdiction of the civil courts, inheritors of the pre-revolutionary *Parlements*. The Law of 16–24 August 1790 famously provides that:

Judicial functions are distinct and will always remain separate from administrative functions. It shall be a criminal offence for the judges of the ordinary courts to interfere in any manner whatsoever with the operation of the administration, nor shall they call administrators to account before them in respect of the exercise of their official functions.

Reinforced by a decree in 1795, which forbids the courts 'to take cognizance of acts of the administration', the provision is still in force.[1] Over the centuries, the state immunity confirmed by this provision was ended by the prestigious Conseil d'Etat, which, during the late nineteenth century, succeeded in turning a previously advisory function into an administrative jurisdiction and establishing it within its hallowed walls. As suggested by the Law of 1790, this jurisdiction came to be viewed as a manifestation of the institutional interpretation of the Separation of Powers doctrine to which France subscribes.[2]

---

[1] For a concise account see L. Neville Brown and J. Bell, *French Administrative Law* (4th edn, Oxford: Oxford University Press, 1993).
[2] On which see M. Troper, *La Séparation des pouvoirs et l'histoire constitutionnelle française* (Paris: LGDJ, 1980).

These historical events set France off in a direction diametrically opposite to that taken by England at the time of the guarantees of the Act of Settlement in 1701.[3] In England, as more formally in the United States, the idea of institutional 'checks and balances' prevailed, making it natural to subject government officials to the jurisdiction of the common law courts, a choice which came to be celebrated by Dicey in his rule of law doctrine with the principle of equality before the law and personal responsibility of government officials to the 'ordinary' courts. The consequence was a rule of personal liability for torts committed by officials in the exercise of public powers.[4] For France, once the immunity of public officials had been established in 1790, this answer was impossible. Consequently, France was to take the opposite road to personal liability, making the state and not the servant liable for wrongs committed in the name of a public service.

The *Blanco* decision, which finally established the jurisdiction of the Conseil d'Etat[5] in liability cases, is considered sufficiently influential to stand first in the collection of 'Great Cases of French Administrative Law'.[6] The case involved a simple traffic accident: a child had been run down by a wagon owned by a tobacco factory, a state monopoly. The father brought an action in damages under the liability sections of the Civil Code in the ordinary courts, whose jurisdiction was contested. The Tribunal des Conflits, which exists to decide disputes over competence, ruled that the administrative jurisdiction had competence in the case.[7] At least from the viewpoint of an outsider, this is

---

[3] J. Allison, *A Continental Distinction in the Common Law, A Historical and Comparative Perspective on English Public Law* (Oxford: Clarendon, paperback edition, 2000) at 152–7.

[4] Confirmed by *Entick v Carrington* (1765) 2 Wils. KB 275; *Leach v Money* (1765) 19 St. Tr. 1001; *Wilkes v Wood* (1763) 2 Wils. KB 203.

[5] Today this jurisdiction is largely delegated to departmental administrative tribunals and appeal tribunals: see Brown and Bell, above note 1.

[6] TC 8 February 1873 *Blanco* Rec. 1er supplement 61, concl David; M. Long *et al.*, *Les Grands arrêts de la jurisprudence administrative* (10th edn, Paris: Sirey, 1990) (hereafter GA) No 1.

[7] Strictly, the term 'jurisdiction' is inappropriate here, as the Conseil d'Etat still had purely advisory functions and the judgment uses the term '*autorité administrative*'.

perhaps not a highly significant ruling. Indeed, the jurisdictional aspects of the decision were ultimately to provoke legislative intervention; today, the *Blanco* case would be handled by the civil courts, to which jurisdiction in all traffic accident cases was transferred in 1957.

The true significance of *Blanco* for the future of administrative liability lay in the Tribunal's reasoning. It was asserted in the judgment that:

The responsibility, which may accrue to the State for losses caused to individuals in respect of persons employed in the public service, cannot be regulated by the principles set out in the Civil Code in respect of relationships between individuals;

This responsibility is neither general, nor absolute; it has special rules, which vary according to the needs of the service and the necessity for reconciling the rights of the State with private rights; For this reason, together with the terms of the relevant laws, the administrative authority is alone competent to hear such cases.

In the instant case, the insistence on the necessity for *special rules* of liability was surely contestable; the case after all involved an accident with a horse and cart. It was this reasoning, however, that later proved so attractive to British scholars, concerned at what they saw as the specially lenient treatment accorded to public authorities by the English courts in judging cases of civil liability once the doctrine of Crown immunity had finally been abolished by the Crown Proceedings Act of 1947.[8]

It is not my purpose in this brief Annex to give an account or attempt an evaluation of the system of state liability developed by the French administrative courts. The dual jurisdiction is undoubtedly complex, and a high price is paid in boundary disputes. As I have already stated, to graft this system on to the English common law judicial system is not in my view a political runner. It is my personal belief that it is healthy for the state and its officials to be, as

---

[8] In particular by J. D. M. Mitchell, 'The Causes and Effects of the Absence of a System of Public Law in the United Kingdom' [1965] *PL* 95 but see also C. J. Hamson, 'Escaping Borstal Boys and the Immunity of Office' [1969] *Cam. LJ* 273.

they are in the common law system, accountable to the ordinary civil law system administered by the ordinary civil courts. Dicey's equality principle, when it was written, captured a fundamental attitude towards government and continues to reflect a political ideal of equality widely adhered to throughout the common law world;[9] in an age of democratic and supposedly accountable government, it has 'immediate intuitive appeal'.[10] At a more pragmatic level, I see the introduction of separate rules of liability based on a public/private distinction as an unnecessary complication and, to reiterate, 'wilfully to throw away the advantages of our flexible, unitary jurisdiction'.[11]

To break with our established constitutional tradition very strong justification is needed. Justification could be found if the separate French system of administrative liability produced results greatly superior to those evolved by the common law. The academic observers who, during the 1970s, argued that the change should be made, believed themselves to be looking at a system that was doctrinally greatly superior. They saw the French liability system as tough on public authorities and British judges as overprotective of public funds. They also saw problems with the doctrine of vicarious liability introduced as the basis of Crown liability by the Crown Proceedings Act of 1947 and felt that these could be circumvented by the concept of *faute de service*, after *Blanco* the focal point of French administrative liability. Today, the common law has devised its own internal solutions to these problems, by resort to notions of non-delegable and statutory duty,[12] solutions that bear a strong resemblance to the French notion of *faute de service*. The common law observers were also attracted by the fact that French administrative law operates a stepped liability

---

[9] P. Hogg, *The Liability of the Crown* (2nd edn, Toronto: Carswell, 1989) at 1–2.

[10] D. Mullan, 'Book Review, The Liability of the Crown' (1990) 10 *Windsor Yearbook of Access to Justice* 263, 264.

[11] This position was argued contemporaneously in C. Harlow, '"Public" and "Private" Law: Definition Without Distinction' (1980) 43 *MLR* 241.

[12] Above Chap. 1, text at notes 30–31.

system: the test for liability varies from gross fault, through the civil law standard of simple fault, to no-fault liability. It should, however, be borne in mind in considering the apparent advantage of the stepped system that French civil law makes greater use of strict liability (as, for example, risk liability for hazardous activity[13]) than common law systems and also acknowledges a principle of abuse of rights.[14]

Further inquiry has shown that, in practice if not in theory, the similarities between English and French administrative law are greater than the differences. Thus Fairgrieve, author of the leading comparative monograph, recently concluded:[15]

the two systems are not as divergent as one might have thought. Outcomes can often be very similar, and the legal concepts used to reach them are not always dissimilar.... In practical terms, the finding of fault is influenced by similar factors in both countries, such as foreseeability of loss and the complexity of the impugned activity.... A similarity is also found in the common need to keep state liability within reasonable limits.

Suffice it to say that, from my limited knowledge of the two systems, I believe this conclusion to be correct.

This is not the place for an extended survey of administrative liability in France. It is, however, noticeable that the very same issues that have proved so problematic in a common law context have equally beleaguered the French courts, both civil and administrative. Indeed, the globalization phenomenon referred to in my second lecture has meant that courts are increasingly faced in one jurisdiction after another, with the very same 'hard cases'. To take a single example, courts throughout the world have been asked to award 'damages for wrongful birth' in cases where a pregnancy has resulted after an unsuccessful

[13] Thus the celebrated case of the CE *Regnault-Desroziers* 28 March 1919, S 1918. III. 25 n. Hauriou, which establishes risk liability for hazardous activities, closely resembles the equally celebrated civil case of *Jandheur*, imposing liability for a fire in a department store.

[14] C. Harlow, *Compensation and Government Torts* (London: Sweet and Maxwell, 1982) at 58–68.

[15] D. Fairgrieve, *State Liability in Tort* (Oxford: Oxford University Press, 2002) at 260–1.

sterilization operation.[16] The solutions arrived at naturally vary: cultural assumptions and values vary and a hard case is always a hard case.

Other very direct parallels exist in situations discussed in the text of my lectures. In France as in England, for example, there has recently been a spate of cases involving the liability of rescue services, leading on both sides of the Channel to extensions of liability.[17] It is interesting, too, to note that leading French commentators have pointed to the difficulty of weighing the needs of the administration when the preservation of human life is in the balance. They conclude that, across the board, the reservation of liability to cases of grave fault will not be adhered to in such cases.[18] This is much the same idea as that contained in the 'vulnerable victim' concept so influential in the common law. No doubt Atiyah's 'blame culture' is also operative in France, where the same strong financial incentives exist to blame others for loss or death or wrongful injury. Again, it is notable how, in cases where economic loss has arisen through the operation of a regulator, both systems have shown themselves much more cautious.[19]

---

[16] For France, see Cass Civ, Ass Plen 17 November 2000 *Perruche* D. 2001 Juris 332; JCP 2001.II.10438. In the eyes of the legislature, the civil courts got the answer 'wrong', provoking Law No 2002–303 (4 March 2002), noted by Deguerge, *AJDA* 2002.508. For Australia, see *Cattanach v Melchior* [2003] HCA 38 (16 July 2003) where the Australian High Court was critical of the House of Lords decision in the similar case of *Rees v Darlington Memorial Hospital NHS Trust* [2003] 3 WLR 1091.

[17] For France, see CE 29 April 1998 *Commune de Hannapes* RDP 1998. 1012; for England, see *John Munroe (Acrylics) Ltd v London Fire and Civil Defence Authority* [1996] 3 WLR 988; *Capital & Counties plc v Hampshire CC* [1997] 2 All ER 865.

[18] *AJDA* 2002.133 chr Guyomar and Collin at 136.

[19] E.g., in CE 30 November 2001 *Kechichin* AJDA 2002.133 concl Seban note Guyomar and Collin, there is talk of a 'balancing test', in which the 'nature, difficulty and needs of public service' are weighed against the interests of the victim. For England, compare *Three Rivers District Council v Governor and Company of the Bank of England* [2000] 2 WLR 1227, arguably halting the attrition of tests for liability in the tort of misfeasance in public office. See M. Andenas and D. Fairgrieve, 'Misfeasance in Public Office, Governmental Liability and European Influences' (2002) 51 *ICLQ* 757.

Whether or not the principles and application of French civil and administrative law to tort cases really differ significantly has always been hotly debated and is in any event a question for French commentators.[20] Recent French experience shows how hard it is to resist pressure to standardize liability tests. Problems have arisen in particular in medical liability cases, where a direct comparison between public and private hospitals is possible. Cases brought to the courts in the aftermath of the notorious 'affair of contaminated blood', concerning infection with the HIV virus through blood transfusions, showed that two separate jurisdictions and four possible grounds of liability were in place, a situation leading to risk of serious inequality.[21] It was not until 1999, after an influential report from the Conseil d'Etat,[22] that the courts felt free to experiment with the precautionary principle as a basis for liability, borrowed from environmental law. Further complexity was introduced by the intervention of the European Union to harmonize products liability regulation.[23]

Nothing that has been said here is to be read as critical of the French system of administrative liability, of which I am a great admirer. All I am saying is that courts throughout the world are being faced with liability claims of great

---

[20] The leading modern study is by C. Eisenmann, 'Sur le degré d'originalité du régime de responsabilité extra-contractuelle des personnes (collectivités) publiques' *JCP* 1949.I.742 and 751. For a thoughtful, theoretical comparison see D. Lochak, 'Réfléxion sur les functions sociales de la responsibilité administrative' in CURRAP, *Le Droit administratif* (Paris: PUF, 1993).

[21] The problems are discussed in the leading case of CE 26 May 1995 (Ass) *Consorts N'Guyen, Joaun, Consorts Pavan* RFDA 1995.748 concl Daël. And see Pontier, 'SIDA et responsabilité: problèmes de droit public' *RFDA* 1992.533.

[22] *Rapport Public* 1998: *Droit de Santé.*

[23] G. Howells and M. Mildred, 'Infected Blood: Defect and Discoverability, A First Exposition of the EC Product Liability Directive' (2002) 65 *MLR* 95. EC law has also had an unfavourable impact on the French law of products liability: see Case C–52/00 *Commission v France*, C–154/00 *Commission v Greece*, C–193/00 *González Sánchez v Medicina Asturiana* [2002] ELR I–3827, where the ECJ ruled that product liability law is a maximum standard of harmonization, from which there can be no deviation, even in the interests of claimants.

difficulty in situations of increasing regulatory complexity. Not only is legislation growing textually more complex and less transparent but regulation is increasingly penetrative and intrusive. Just as the private and public sectors are moving closer together so the national and transnational are converging. There is too, increasingly, resort to international conventions. Additional jurisdictional complexity is introduced into both systems of domestic law by EC law, which crosses the public/private border and also by the European Court of Human Rights, to which all jurisdictions are now subject. As I have argued in my second lecture, the state and its national legal system are no longer internally omnipotent. They are subject to global influences and 'forum shopping' practices. Internally and externally, there has been a constant blurring of the public/private divide. This context is a context in which separate rules and deviant standards of liability can only add to the prevailing confusion. French courts, administrative and civil, are equally susceptible to these external influences, with their integrative stresses. They cannot fail to be conscious of the fact.

# Index

Accident compensation
  schemes 2, 91–105, 131
  globalization and 45
  New Zealand 95–100, 101
Accountability 34, 35, 37, 122
  liability and 49–53
Administrative compensation
  88–123
  accident compensation
    schemes 2, 91–105, 131
  compensation as good
    administration 105–9
  general principle of
    compensation 116–23
Administrative law, France
  134–41
Affirmative remedies 44, 77,
  85, 86, 124
Affirmative rights 44, 124
Agent Orange case 46
Aggravated damages 107
Aggregative political
  principles 3, 4
Alder Hey Hospital case 121–2
Archaeological sites 34
Asbestos cases 47–8
Asylum seekers 83, 113–14
Atiyah, Patrick 7, 13, 22, 30, 62,
  90–1, 95, 113, 121, 139
Atkin, Lord 18

Banking, supervision of 36–7
Barlow Clowes case 109
Barry, Brian 3
Bathing water quality 64–5

Benchmarking 133
Bhopal disaster 45–6, 50
Bingham, Lord 14
Blame/culpability 17, 22–3
  international law and 53–4
'Botheration payments' 106–7,
  113, 120
BSE crisis 89
Buckley, R. A. 33–4
Burden of proof, negligence
  cases 15
Burns, P. 15, 16

Calabresi, Guido 15
Camelford case 51, 131
Canadian Charter of
  Fundamental Rights
  and Freedoms 77
Cane, Peter 3–4, 11, 13–14,
  90–1, 113, 116–18, 123
Caranta, Roberto 57–8
Care, duty of see Duty of care
Carnwarth, Robert 2
Cascade effect 58, 90
Causation 12
Children
  abuse 29–30, 84–5
  guardian ad litem 82
  organ retention (Alder Hey
    Hospital case) 121–2
  poverty and 82–3
  special needs education
    27–8, 83–4, 120
  statutory child care 75–6,
    81–2, 84

statutory protection of 28, 30
thalidomide cases 94
United Nations Convention
on the Rights of the
Child 80
Children and Family Court
Advisory service
(CAFCAS) 82
Citizen's Charters 4–5
Civil liability, general principle
of 18
Class actions 46–9, 52–3, 90,
103
accountability through
liability 49–53
Cohen, David 1, 3, 5, 12, 30, 38,
93, 118, 120
Collective consumption 119,
124–33
Commission for Local
Administration 106,
113
Compensation 8, 22
accident compensation 2,
91–105, 131
administrative 88–123
accident compensation
schemes 2, 91–105
compensation as good
administration 105–9
general principle of
compensation 116–23
Administrative Court and
115–16
'botheration payments'
106–7, 113, 120
conduct and 12
criminal injuries
compensation 76, 89,
100–2
culture of 4, 6, 90, 91, 121,
125, 126, 127

damage caused by
absconders from prison
18
*ex gratia* 88, 89, 106, 122
French law and 60–1, 71
general principle of 109,
116–23
German law and 59–60
human rights and 68, 76,
109–16
identification of 88–91
international law and 55
just satisfaction and 68–85,
110
*restitutio in integrum* 69, 71
as tort tax 14–22
Consent, defence in negligence
cases 13
Consumerism 5, 8, 41, 52
Contract, privity of 17
Contracting out 35
Cooke, Lord 19
Corrective justice 10–41, 44, 79,
126
class actions and 48
compensation as tort tax
14–22
culpability/blame and 17,
22–3
deterrence 23–30
taking Dicey seriously 30–41
Courts
Administrative Court 115–16
European Court of Human
Rights (ECtHR) 42,
68–85, 110, 141
European Court of Justice
42, 56–67
Criminal injuries
compensation 76,
89, 100–2
Crown 1, 22, 38–9, 88, 136

Culpability *see* Blame/ culpability

Damage
 nervous shock 50
 property 17–18
Damages 8, 22, 30
 aggravated 107
 deterrent 78
 economic loss 19
 exemplary 24, 71, 131
 human rights cases 76–7, 111–15
 mental distress 106–7
 'penalty payments' and 63–4
 perverse incentives and 24
 punitive 27
 *restitutio in integrum* 69, 71
 wrongful birth and 138–9
Danger, failure to warn of 20–1
Decision-making
 'decision traps' 26, 27, 28, 79, 111
 policy element 38
 polycentric 27, 28
 studies of effect of tort law on 28–30
Declaration of incompatibility 109
Detention of foreign nationals 55
Deterrence 78–9
 deterrent damages 78
 Dicey on 23–4, 30–41, 79
 tort law as 23–30, 127
Dicey, Albert Venn 12
 deterrence and 23–4, 30–41, 79
 equality and 6, 22, 135, 137
 personal liability and 23, 41
 personal responsibility and 135

rule of law and 22, 79, 135
 statutory powers and 23
Disability, housing and 112–13
Discrimination 56
Dispute settlement procedures 56
Distributive justice 2–3, 13, 85, 116, 118, 124, 126
 affirmative rights and 44
 public law and 3–4
 security and 6
Duty of care 11, 37
 as control device 18–19
 general 16
 non-delegable 17
 statutory protection of children and 30

Economic loss 19
Economic rationalism 24–5
Education, special needs 27–8, 83–4, 120
Empirical analysis and evidence 25–6, 93–4
England, Ishtak 2
Entitlement theory of state liability 3, 118, 120
Environmental issues 28, 33
 bathing water quality 64–5
 Bhopal disaster 45–6, 50
 Camelford case 51, 131
 environmental accidents 26
 EU environmental liability regime 65
 waste disposal 64
Equality before public charges 60, 71
Equality before the law 6–7, 22, 135, 137
Ethics, international law and 53–4

European Convention on
   Human Rights 68, 76,
   110, 112, 113, 132
   Article 3 (torture and
   inhuman treatment)
   70–1, 77
   fair hearing right 73–5
   friendly settlement
   procedure 70–1
European Court of Human
   Rights (ECtHR) 42, 110,
   141
   friendly settlement
   procedure 70–1
   just satisfaction and 68–85,
   110
   reparation and 69–71
European Union (EU) 141
   European Court of Justice
   (ECJ) 42, 56–67
   liability and 56–67
   product liability 52
   milk quotas 67, 89
   penalty payment procedure
   63–4
   product liability and 52
   *Schöppenstedt* formula
   58–9, 60
*Ex gratia* compensation 88, 89,
   106, 122
Exemplary damages 24, 71, 131

Fair hearing right 73–5
Fairgreave, D. 138
Fault *see* Blame/culpability
*Faute de service* 137–8
Feldthusen, B. 38
Fishing regulation 107–8
Fleming, John 7, 47, 49
Foreseeability 18, 19
Forum shopping 46
France

administrative law 134–41
   compensation in 60–1, 71
   Conseil d'Etat 134, 135, 140
   *faute de service* 137–8
   medical negligence in 140
*Francovich* liability 56–8, 62–7
Freeman, J. 31
Functionalism 7, 8, 10–11, 13,
   25–6, 62

Gaudron J 37
Germany, compensation in
   59–60
Globalization 138
   accident compensation and
   45
   cascade effect of 42–9
Goff, Lord 19
Guardian *ad litem* 82
Gulf War cases 51, 103–4

Health care, inadequacy of 21
Higgins, Rosalyn 53–4, 57
Hillsborough disaster 50
Hoffmann, Lord 32–3, 34, 40
Hogg, Peter 22, 133
Housing 112–14
   asylum seekers 113–14
   temporary 119–20
Huber, P. 15
Human rights 8, 41, 42, 79–80,
   107
   affirmative 44
   compensation and 68, 76,
   109–16
   competing 27
   damages and 111–15
   Human Rights Act 1988
   (HRA) 29, 76, 81,
   109–10, 112, 114, 116, 132
   legalism and 8
   negative rights 118

Human rights (*Continued*)
  torture and inhuman
      treatment prohibition
      70–1, 77
  Van Boven Report 55
  *see also* European
      Convention on Human
      Rights; European Court
      of Human Rights

Injunctions 86
Instrumentalism 7
Insurance 21, 25, 40, 127–8, 129
International law 6
  compensation and 55
  ethics and 53–4
  globalization and 42–9
  remedies 54–6
  reparation and 54–5
  strict liability and 54
International Law Commission
      (ILC) 54, 55
Interventionist state 31, 41
Ipp Committee 127–8, 129, 132

Jennings, I. W. 23
Judicial review 23, 34, 94
Just satisfaction 68–85, 110

Klar, L. 98

Law Commission 24, 71, 107,
      132
Leapfrogging of intermediary
      parties 16, 20
Legal transplants 43
Limitation periods 74
Litigation, overuse of 8
Local authorities 62–3
  Commission for Local
      Administration 106, 113
  housing and *see* Housing

statutory child care 75–6,
      81–2, 84
Loss, corrective justice and
      12–13

Maladministration 72, 109
  'botheration payments'
      106–7, 113, 120
  compensation for 106
Mass litigation *see* Class
      actions
Mediation 115
Medical (clinical) negligence
      102–3
  France 140
Mental distress 106–7
  nervous shock 50
Mental Health Review
      Tribunals 112
Merits of cases 29
Milk quotas 67, 89
Miller, D. 126
Ministry of Defence cases
      49–50, 51, 103–4
Misfeasance in public office
      36–7, 130–1

National Audit Office (NAO)
      102, 103
National Health Service (NHS)
      35, 102, 127
Negative remedies 44
Negative rights 118
Negligence
  burden of proof 15
  consent defence 13
  economic loss and 19
  in exercise of statutory child
      care 75–6
  as failure of control 16
  'fair, just and reasonable'
      test 73

foreseeability 19
medical (clinical) negligence 102–3, 140
omission to act and 16, 39–40
operational 38
police 72–3, 77–9
public law duty 75–6
statutory protection of children 28
systemic breakdown and 24
welfare state and 126
Neighbour principle 15, 18
Nervous shock 50
New Zealand accident compensation scheme 95–100, 101
Nicholls, Lord 32, 39, 40, 130
No-fault liability 95, 96, 138
Non-delegable duty 137
Nuisance 32

Ogus, A. 107
Oliver, Dawn 51, 124–5
Ombudsman 72, 89, 115, 122
Commission for Local Administration 106, 113
Parliamentary 106–9
tort law as 51, 73
Omission to act, liability for 16, 39–40
Operational negligence 38
Organ retention (Alder Hey Hospital case) 121–2
Out-of-court settlements 26

Palmer, Sir Geoffrey 99
Parity principle 34, 41, 128
Parliamentary Commissioner for Administration (PCA) 106–9

Pearson Commission on Civil Liability for Personal Injuries 94–5, 127
Penalty payment procedure 63–4
Personal injuries 128
sport and 128–9
Personal liability doctrine 22–3
Perverse incentives, damages and 24
Planning legislation 89
Police 26–7, 50, 104–5
negligence 72–3, 77–9
Posner, Richard 15
Preventive action, failure to take 16
Privatization, public/private boundary and 31–6
Privity, abolition of 17
Product liability 52–3
EU law and 52
globalization and 45–6
strict liability 15, 45
tobacco cases 52–3
United States 15, 45
Proof, burden of 15
Property, damage to 17–18
Prosser, T. 38
Public authorities
failure to exercise powers 16
illegality and 110
liabilities of 1
regulation by *see* Regulation
statutory duty and 132
statutory powers 23, 37, 39
Public law, distributive justice and 3–4
Public/private boundary 31–40, 130
Punitive damages 27

Quality, defects in 19

Rail industry 34, 35–6
Rape, police negligence and 77–9
Rationalism, economic 24–5
Regional authorities 62–3
Regulation 6, 13, 20, 21, 23
  banking supervision 36–7
  compensation claims and 52
  failure of 126
Reid, Lord 18, 19, 129
Reid, William 106
Reliance, generalized 5
Remedies
  affirmative 44, 77, 85, 86
  declaration of incompatibility 109
  globalization and 44
  Human Rights Act 109–10
  injunctions 86
  international law 54–6
  negative 44, 77, 85
  public law 114–15
  *see also* Damages
Reparation 13, 69–71
  international law and 54–5
Rescue services 139
Reservations in treaties 56
Resources
  allocation of 12, 28, 80, 116, 119–20, 126
  liability and 11
Responsibility 124, 135
  liability and 53–6
*Restitutio in integrum* 69, 71
Ripstein, A. 22
Risk 117
  aversion to 5–6, 16, 90, 125–6, 127
  risk-proofing 21
Rule of law 22, 79, 135
Rule-making functions 36

Salmonella in eggs 89
Sanction theory of tort law 57–8
*Schöppenstedt* formula 58–9, 60
Schuck, Peter 24–6, 30
*Schutznormtheorie* 59–60
Schwartz, Gary 15
Security 6, 125
Selective comparison process 62
Sexual offences 27
Smith, J. 118, 120
Smith, J. C. 15, 16
Social security *see* Welfare state
Social solidarity 93, 126
Social workers 27–8, 84
Special needs education 27–8, 83–4, 120
Spigelman, J. J. 5, 126
Sport, personal injuries and 128–9
Standards in public life 23
Stapleton, Jane 8, 16–17, 18, 21
Statutory duty 132, 137
  child care 75–6, 81–2, 84
  child protection 28, 30
Steyn, Lord 130
Strict liability 54, 95, 138
  product liability 15, 45
'Striking out' procedure 75

Taxation 25
Temporary housing 119–20
Terrorism 48–9
Thalidomide cases 94
Tobacco cases 52–3
Tomuschat, Christian 55–6, 66, 87
Tort law 4, 5
  compensation as tort tax 14–22
  conceptual bases 8

corrective justice and 10–41
as deterrent 23–30, 127
effectiveness 7
globalization and 42–9
objectivity of 11
as Ombudsman 51, 73
retraction of 132–3
sanction theory of 57–8
studies of effect on decision-
    making 28–30
success of 21
Torture and inhuman
    treatment prohibition
    70–1, 77
Traffic accidents 25–6, 39–40,
    135–6
Treaties, reservations 56
Trespass 23–4, 34

United Nations
Committee on the Rights of
    the Child 82–3
Convention on the Rights of
    the Child 80
Covenant on Civil and
    Political Rights 55
Human Rights Committee
    56, 80
Van Boven Report 55
United States, product liability
    in 15, 45

Vaccine damage cases 93–4
Van Boven Report 55
Van Gerven, Walter 57, 58
Vicarious liability 17
Victims
    accident compensation
        schemes 2, 91–105,
        131
    changing attitudes to 15
    class actions by *see* Class
        actions
    criminal injuries
        compensation 76, 89,
        100–2
    expectations 19
    vulnerable 21, 30

Water authorities 31–5
Weinrib, Ernest 10–11, 14
Welfare state 4, 23, 41,
    96
    discrimination in 56
    distributive justice and 2
    negligence and 126
Wells, Celia 49
Whiplash effect 65, 67
Woolf, Lord 110–11, 114
World Trade Organization 42,
    66
Writ, action begun by 115–16
Wrongful birth 138–9

Printed in the United Kingdom
by Lightning Source UK Ltd.
129569UK00001B/48/A